LABOR
STATISTICS
and
CLASS
STRUGGLE

Marc Linder

International Publishers **New York**

Library of Congress Cataloging-in-Publication Data

Linder, Marc.
    Labor statistics and class struggle / Marc Linder.
        p.   cm.
    Includes bibliographical references and index.
    ISBN 0-7178-0711-8 : $7.50
    1. Labor costs--Statistics--History. 2. Labor supply--Statistics-
-History. 3. Industrial accidents--Statistics--History.   I. Title.
HD4909.L53   1994
331.1--dc20   94-34677
                                                                CIP

CONTENTS

Illustrations

Preface

Unlike scholarly perception of the administrative process, which high jurisprudential authority has characterized as "no more conservative or liberal than the elevator in the Senate Office Building,"[1] economists at times have candidly given voice to popular suspicions about the neutrality of statistics[2]: "The selection of a particular index out of several, or even the question of which prices to include . . . is part of the political power struggle."[3]

Such skepticism toward the political origins, design, collection, and uses of economic data is in part based on the insight that counting methods embody assumptions about the objects of enumeration.[4] In spite of this burgeoning epistemological awareness, economists and historians have devoted little attention to tracing the ideologies underlying individual statistical series. Even where scholars have succeeded in peeling off the imperial raiments that methodologically shroud venerable and seemingly straightforward data, they have often failed to penetrate beyond explanations that focus on bureaucratic inertia.[5]

The following exemplary social histories of statistical politics deal with two series that reflect core aspects of the antagonistic relationship between labor and capital. The first, unit labor costs, captures, albeit distortedly, the income-related outcome of struggles over exploitation. The second, workplace deaths, sheds light on the fatal costs imposed by the process of extraction of surplus from workers. Whereas the history of the enumeration of industrial fatalities has largely been one of malignant neglect, the course of unit labor costs has been ideologically much more complex and contentious.

Gail Hollander, John Houghton, Harry Magdoff, Andrew Morriss, Victor Perlo, and Larry Zacharias incisively criticized the manuscript; Morriss generated the graphs; and Magdoff, Perlo, and Jürgen Kuczynski generously furnished background information.

LABOR STATISTICS and CLASS STRUGGLE

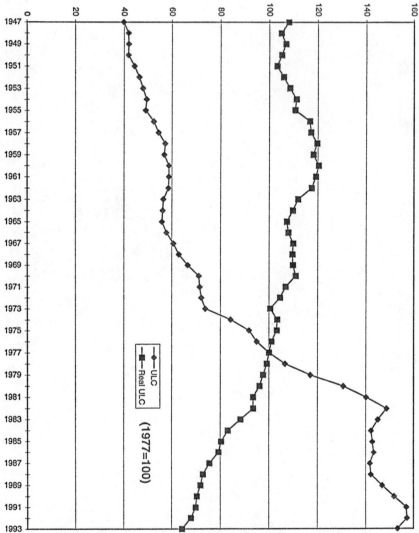

Figure 1: Nominal & Real Unit Labor Costs in Manufacturing, 1947-93

I
From Surplus Value to Unit Labor Costs: The Bourgeoisification of a Communist Conspiracy

[N]either nominal wages, i.e. the sum of money for which the worker sells himself to the capitalist, nor real wages, i.e. the sum of commodities which he can buy for this money, exhaust the relations contained in the wage.

The wage is above all determined by its relationship to the gain, to the profit of the capitalist—comparative, relative wages [Marx 1959, 413].

The American Federation of Labor is the first organization of Labor in the world to realize the importance of the factor productivity in economic society. It no longer strives merely for higher money wages; it no longer strives merely for higher real wages; it strives for *higher social wages*, for wages which increase as measured by prices and *productivity* [Green 1927a, 919–20].

Among the thousands of potential statistical candidates for substantive and methodological scrutiny, the category of unit labor cost(s) (ULC)[1] seems as innocuous as any. Yet the origins and transformations of ULC discourse make it peculiarly appropriate for critical historical analysis. For the path from Marx's proto-conceptualization of exploitation in terms of "relative wages" to the American Federation of Labor's formulation of a "social wage" policy in the 1920s and from there to ULC as an indicator of business well-being and national competitiveness has been tortuous.

The analysis begins with a brief preview of the contemporary official and orthodox economic understandings of ULC as a measure of how much firms must pay out in current (inflated) wages per hour to produce a fixed unit of physical (or deflated) output. ULC is then contrasted with an alternative approach, which, by relating real wages to real output, directs attention to class-distributional income shares. The focus then shifts to the statistical progenitors of ULC. The first way station is the adoption by the conservative American Federation of Labor (AFL) in the 1920s of a collective bargaining wage policy that was based on a notion of labor's share in national income that was suspiciously reminiscent of Marx's original (pre-*Kapital*) analysis of capitalist exploitation. After solving this mystery, the essay examines the methodological contributions during the New Deal and World War II by a small group of U.S. government economists—whom McCarthyites later hounded out of employment—to the creation of the statistical underpinnings of the components of labor's share or ULC. The final part of the account is devoted to the postwar transformation of ULC, which ultimately hegemonized productivity discourse in the service of "neutral" inflation-fighting. This scholarly and popular-propagandistic triumph is shown to have been institutionally forged by the U.S. Bureau of Labor Statistics and the President's Council of Economic Advisers.

In sum, then, as different class interests reconfigured the components used in calculating ULC, the statistic underwent a transformation—from a datum to which workers could appeal to press for a share in the surplus to one that discounted workers' contributions to the surplus through inflation adjustments and supported employers' arguments against wage increases based on low productivity gains.

ULC Today

The bipolar class distribution of income (Y) can be recast in the categories of official national income accounts by reference to the wage (or labor) share (W/Y) and the capital (or property) share (P/Y). If Marx's relationship of the rate of surplus value ("the degree of exploitation of labor power by capital") (Marx 1867, 185) is approximated by (P/Y)/(W/Y) or P/W, then any discussion of labor's share necessarily implicates surplus value extraction. If aggregate real wages (W_r) are divided by the total hours of labor (L), then the real hourly wage (W_r/L) is the result. Similarly, if real national income (X) is divided by L, the resulting magnitude (X/L) represents output per hour of labor or productivity. Finally, if both the numerator and the denominator of labor's share are divided by the total number of hours, the resulting expression, $(W_r/L)/(X/L)$, reveals that labor's share is equivalent to real hourly wages divided by hourly output or productivity (Sherman 1991, 157–58; U.S. BLS 1988, 33). Analysis of the movements of this expression, real ULC (RULC) (Hoffmann 1971, 578), may therefore also implicate social struggles over the class distribution of income and the extraction of surplus (Buchele & Christiansen 1993).[2]

As defined by the U.S. Bureau of Labor Statistics (BLS), ULC "measure the cost of labor input required to produce one unit of output and are derived by dividing compensation in current dollars by output in constant dollars" (U.S. BLS 1992, 80). The full version of ULC as labor compensation per unit of output is arrived at "by dividing compensation per man-hour by output per man-hour." The numerator and denominator are asymmetrical inasmuch as the output is expressed in constant dollars whereas the compensation data derive from "current dollars" (U.S. BLS 1974, 9, 184).[3]

In formulating ULC in this way, economists adopt the perspective of the employer, who "is interested in two things: how much it costs him to hire a man-hour of labor and how much output he is able to obtain from this man-hour" (Reynolds 1949, 326). But because wages are simultaneously incomes to workers and costs of production to employers (Mark & Kahn 1965, 1056), the businessman's microeconomic perspective is transformed into a statistical basis of macroeconomic policy. In particular, the BLS has emphasized that if productivity increases can offset increases in hourly wages, "pressure to increase prices will lessen in a competitive economy" (U.S. BLS 1988, 33). ULC thus synthesize a number of economic dimensions crucial to analyzing aggregate profitability: total labor time, volume of production, productivity, and wages. ULC are therefore commonly viewed as measuring "changes in the competitiveness of a country's total manufacturing" (Artto 1987, 47).

The contrasting trends of ULC and RULC stand out clearly in Figure 1, which presents data for all persons in manufacturing since 1947 (U.S. BLS 1989, 348–50; *Monthly Labor Review* 1994, 93). ULC has moved steadily upwards during the entire postwar period, whereas RULC has declined almost as sharply. To be sure, however, ULC's progress has not been uninterrupted.

Economists consider declining ULC a positive (lagging) business cycle indicator because productivity increases in excess of wage increases during the contraction and early expansion phases point to mounting profits (Moore 1955; Crotty & Rapping 1975, 796–98; Kendrick & Grossman 1980, 90–96). The impact that the Reagan administration's anti-union and anti-labor policies had on ULC, for example, has been touted as the foundation of the cyclical upswing during the 1980s (Cullity 1990).[4]

The cyclicity of ULC has, in effect, been a staple of business cycle theory since Marx theorized the cyclical movements of the rate of surplus value as determined by the accumulation of capital (and, derivatively, unemployment) and conceptualized the functionality of depressions for restoring profitability (Marx 1867, 599–632). In the early part of the twentieth century, Wesley Mitchell revived interest in the class implications of the business cycle. In particular, he called attention to the fact that wage rates rose slowly at the start of a trade revival whereas wholesale prices rose faster than wages. On the productivity side, "the less efficient employees are the first to be discharged after a crisis. Hence the relatively small working forces of depression are the picked troops of the industrial army." At the height of the prosperity phase, however, "the relatively inefficient reserve army of labor is . . . called into service," while overtime is both expensive and "tired labor" so that workers become "unable to accomplish as much work per hour as in less busy seasons." Moreover, "men cannot be induced to work at so fast a pace when employment is abundant as when it is scarce." Consequently, "this combination of advancing prices for labor and declining efficiency produces a serious increase in the cost of getting work done. . . ." (Mitchell 1941, 31–34). During the Great Depression of the 1930s, labor economists also observed that physical output per man-hour "leaped ahead in spectacular fashion" vis-à-vis real wages because inefficient firms and workers were subject to "'weeding out'" while the fear of unemployment spurred the remaining workers to greater efficiency (Mills & Montgomery 1938, 154).

The Reddening of the American Federation of Labor

Since the mid-1920s, when the AFL announced its new wage policy according to which "[s]ocial inequality, industrial instability and injustice must increase unless the workers' real wages . . . are progressed in proportion to man's increasing power of production" (AFL 1925, 271), unions, capital, and the state have sought to develop economic indicators to determine the degree to which labor is achieving this objective and what the macroeconomic consequences of a productivity-centered wage policy are.

This task assumed particular urgency during the "New Capitalism" of the 1920s when "[a] surge . . . in productivity, probably exceeding in its intensity and rivaling in the scope and magnitude of its effects the advance which has given the label of 'industrial revolution' to the events of the late 18th and early 19th centuries in England, was under way" (Mills 1932, 556). Consequently, "physical product . . . leaped ahead of real earnings" (Mills & Montgomery 1938, 152), bringing about "substantial declines in labor costs per unit of product" and causing "profit margins . . . to swell." The fact that "[t]he reward of labor for its contribution to each unit (i.e., labor per unit for goods produced, in dollars of constant purchasing power) was declining" was another way of saying that "[f]or wage earners in manufacturing industries contributions in excess of withdrawals were piled up" (Mills 1932, 397, 550–51, 553). The cumulative result of this redistribution of income from labor to capital, overaccumulation of capital, and overproduction of commodities was the unprecedented Great Depression of the 1930s (Douglas 1930, 504–48; Leven, Moulton, & Warburton 1934, 125–33).[5]

In the midst of this monumental redistribution process, the delegates to the forty-fifth annual convention of the AFL assembled on the boardwalk at Atlantic City in October 1925 voted to approve a new wage policy—and, *The New York Times* certified, "not one Communist was there to dissent" (Clark 1926, 1). The immediate background to their deliberations extended to the wage and price experiences of World War I. War-time union contracts and labor arbitrations had embodied the principle that money wages should increase in tandem with the cost of living. When employers sought to enforce the principle in reverse by demanding wage reductions as prices fell after the War (Soule 1968, 218), the AFL attacked the cost-of-living-centered wage policy as "a violation of the whole philosophy in progress and civilization and . . . utterly without logic or scientific support . . . ." Moreover, the Federation objected to that policy's tendency "to standardize classes, each class having a presumptive right to a given quantity of . . . commodities." Desiring but not yet in a position to formulate a "scientifically sound" policy, the 1921 AFL convention aspired to find a "method of relating standards of living to social usefulness, or production service," and authorized the Executive Council "to conduct an investigation into the whole question of wages and cost of living" (AFL 1921, 68, 314).

The committee that was appointed to investigate failed to meet during the following year because it lacked the funds to survey wage theories. Instead, the committee's executive secretary, Matthew Woll, reported to the 1922 convention "that a wage based solely upon costs of living . . . bears no direct relation to production or service rendered. However, a wage based upon productivity . . . must accept as an initial standard a wage based upon human needs and aspirations . . . without reference to the other considerations that enter into a wage which compensates for productivity. . . ." Nevertheless, Woll stated that productivity should be among the factors forming "the basis for wage increments" (AFL 1922, 34–35).

One wage theory available for elaboration by the labor movement was that of "increased productive efficiency," which had first been unsuccessfully advanced by railway unions in a wage arbitration in 1910 and 1913 to justify higher wages based on increased productivity and profits (Stockett 1918, 129–57; Lauck 1929, 32–40, 160–61). The articulation of productivity-linked wage policy received a more effective impetus at the same time from complaints by the International Association of Machinists, the union representing workers at U.S. navy yards and arsenals. Because they were, as government employees, unable to project the same kind of strike threat that undergirded other unionists' collective bargaining demands, their wages had traditionally been set by reference to those prevailing in neighboring plants; during World War I they were also increased in response to rises in the cost of living. But when postwar wage reductions spread among civilian plants, the Machinists sought a new wage policy (Soule 1968, 218). The House of Representatives promptly held hearings on a bill to create a wage board for employees of navy yards and arsenals that would have been required to take into consideration "[t]he average change in per capita productivity of manufacturing industries in the United States over a period covering the preceding ten years" as well as "[t]he progress made in per capita production in manufactories in the United States since 1900 which has not already been reflected in increased wages" (U.S. House of Representatives 1922, 1).

These provisions of the bill, which the AFL supported (AFL 1923, 305–306), were based on a study, commissioned by the Machinists, and carried out by Labor Bureau, Inc., under the direction of the economist George Soule, whom at his death a half-century later *The New York Times* still recalled as a believer in socializing the means of production ("George H. Soule" 1970). In his "Report on the Relation Between Wages and Production," which was appended to the hearings, Soule, waiving for the time being the contention that "the present wage basis does not represent a sufficiently large share of the Nation's income," argued that in order to maintain the workers' current share, real wages would have to be increased by the ten-year moving average increase in production per wage earner (designed to avoid violent fluctuations in wages) (U.S. House of Representatives 1922, 28–29). By publishing condensed versions of his recommendation and data on production, real wages, and wage shares in leading social science journals in 1922 and 1923, Soule was able to promote a broader public discussion of productivity-linked wage policy (Soule 1922; Soule 1923).

Soule's Labor Bureau, Inc. devoted special attention to the issue in its new periodical, *Facts for Workers*, which immediately announced that "even . . . the most conservative economic doctrine" justified unions' demands for wages that took into account the workers' increased productivity ("Does Hard Work Bring More Pay?" 1923). After pointing out that real wages can be increased by maintaining a constant share of a larger product, a larger share of the same product, or a larger share of a larger product, the newsletter, which noted that the share of wages in manufacturing value added had in fact been declining in the twentieth century, made no effort to conceal the zero-sum class conflict inherent in Soule's approach:

> Under capitalist production there is a more or less definite limit to the share workers can obtain, though where that limit is has not been ascertained. There is certainly no reason to believe that the share of the other productive factors . . . cannot be diminished without injury to the economic structure, even on the assumption that the capitalist order is the ultimate form of economic organization ["Wage Theories and Arguments" 1924, 1].

By the time of its 1925 convention, the AFL's Committee on Resolutions, in response to the Executive Council's report, which opposed wage

reductions in the textile industry on the grounds that they reflected wasteful management and would contribute to depression, urged workers to
oppose reductions everywhere and managers to reduce waste. John Frey
of the Molders' Union, "a stanch conservative, [who] frequently concen-
trated his fire on radicals within labor more readily than upon employers"
("John P. Frey Dies" 1957), then moved to amend the Committee's report
by adding the following sentence: "Social inequality, industrial instability
and injustice must increase unless the workers' real wage, the purchasing
power of their wages, is advanced in proportion to man's increasing pow-
ers of production." Frey's purpose was to induce the union movement to
define its wage philosophy beyond vague phrases such as "a fair day's
wage for a fair day's work," "a living wage," or "a full return for the
value of his services to society." A sharp debate ensued, in the course of
which Woll, an AFL vice-president and Republican who had been Gompers' choice as his successor, argued against adoption of Frey's "productive wage theory" on the ground that the AFL should not commit itself
to one single theory. Indeed, for Woll, "the less we have to do with theory
in these matters the better off we are, because . . . our crude judgment
expressed in trade union movement activities has gained more for us."
When Frey failed to accede to Woll's demand for modification, the matter
was referred back to committee, which recommended adoption of Frey's
amendment, which was then unanimously approved (AFL 1925, 36,
231–33, 271).

William Green, the organization's new president and "an uncompli-
cated intellectual mediocrity" (Bernstein 1966, 96), immediately began
devoting himself to explaining the new policy. In an address in January
1926 before the Chicago Forum, Green, speaking "as a member of the
Baptist Church and not as a labor leader," insisted that:

> Labor . . . contends that labor's reward shall not be merely enough to
> meet the requirements of the family budget, but that, in addition, it shall
> be representative, in full measure, of labor's contribution to industry.
> This shifts the whole wage basis from the places where it has been
> erroneously placed, namely, the cost of living, a living wage or a saving
> wage. All of these bases are too intangible, too, indefinite, and too susceptible
> to conflicting interpretations.
> The developments of modern industry have inevitably placed the basis
> of wage demands and wage theories upon the eternal principles of equity,
> justice, fair dealing and frankness ["Asks High Standard" 1926].

The next month Green told Princeton University undergraduates that
if firms failed to pay workers real wages sufficient "'to buy back the
commodities they produce . . . industry will be confronted with a surplus
of idle goods'" ("New Wage Theory" 1926). After the AFL Executive

Council confirmed its commitment to the new "cultural wage" (AFL 1926, 47), Green added this gloss to the AFL's new *Weltanschauung* in an editorial in the AFL's monthly magazine, which *The New York Times* thought important enough to report as news ("Says Labor Enters New Pay Fight Era" 1927):

> In the earliest period organized labor struggled for *higher money wages*.
> A second period in the wage policy began as organized labor realized that the amount of money is no adequate measure for deciding whether a wage is high or low, and that it is necessary to relate money wages to prices. Then organized labor struggled for *higher real wages*—that is, wages that would buy more.
> Very obvious changes in prices induced organized labor to realize the necessity for calculating in real wages.
> Very obvious changes in productivity of labor today induce organized labor again to widen its wage policy.
> Higher money wages from an economic point of view do not improve the situation of the worker if prices increase more than money wages.
> Higher real wages from a social point of view do not improve the situation of the worker if productivity increases more than real wages.
> For higher productivity without corresponding increase of real wages means that the additional product has to be bought by others than the wage-earner. This means that the social position of the wage-earner in relation to other consumers becomes worse . . . [Green 1927a, 919].

Although it is implausible that Green consciously sought aid in Karl Marx's theoretical defense of trade union wage demands, his language was strongly reminiscent of the reasoning that Marx had used in an address to the General Council of the First International in 1865 to refute the claims of one of its members, a carpenter named John Weston, that a general increase of wage rates did not benefit the working class. In discussing the case of an increase in productivity that cheapened a worker's "necessaries" so that after a wage reduction his real wages remained unchanged, Marx said: "Although the labourer's absolute standard of life would have remained the same, his *relative* wages, and, therewith, his *relative social position*, as compared to that of the capitalist, would have been lowered" (Marx 1992, 178).[6] The Marx-AFL real-relative wage policy was thus designed at the very least to make workers whole vis-à-vis increases in prices and productivity.

Green's inability to explain how such "eternal principles" were any less "indefinite" than the earlier "erroneous" ones may have been rooted in the underdeveloped state of productivity data and hence of ULC (Clague 1927, 285): "Since economists were just beginning to construct indices of man-hour output, the Federation could do little more than endorse the general principle" (Bernstein 1966, 103). Rather than by a new-found appreciation of Marxism, the AFL's turn from real to real-relative or "social" wages (AFL 1927a, 29–31) may have been primarily motivated by the decline in consumer prices during the 1920s, "which robbed the old cost-of-living argument of all its efficacy" (McKelvey 1974, 92 n.33; National Industrial Conference Board 1926, 14; U.S. Bureau of the Census 1975, ser. E 135 at 211). Indeed, it was precisely employers' continuing ability to turn the cost-of-living argument against labor that led union leaders to "cast about for some sword to wield in wage disputes that was not double-edged" (Clark 1925, 1).

Whatever the AFL's motivation may have been, Frey, the driving force behind its adoption of the new wage policy, proudly announced that the National City Bank of New York, "this most conservative bank," had informed its clients that the Federation's policy correctly perceived that "'industrial progress'" depended on "'a constant increase in the buying power of the masses'" because ultimately "'everything produced in all of the industries must be sold back to the people engaged in the industries'" (Frey 1926, 34). Indeed, by the next year, Frey euphorically asserted that "no new conception of dealing with a problem has received such international recognition in such a short space of time as" the AFL's new wage policy (AFL 1927b, 195). To be sure, Frey failed to mention that the bank, like the editors of *The New York Times* ("Wage Theory and Practice" 1926), had asserted that capitalism had always operated according to this principle:

> Questions may be raised as to the relative distribution between proprietors and employes, but the proprietors are not running their works on the theory that they are selling their products to each other. . . . Therefore, there can be no controversy over the proposition that "real wages" . . . "must increase in proportion to man's increasing power to [sic] production." It is the basic principle of the existing order of society. . . . It is a declaration in favor of just what has been taking place ever since capital began to be used for increasing production [National City Bank of New York 1925, 192].

What intrigued National City Bank, an ally of J.P. Morgan and Co. (Corey 1934, 413), was not the anti-crisis potential of a social wage policy, but the possibility that the AFL craft unions, abandoning their shop-floor interference with managerial control, might be "inspired to cooperate" in expanding production and productive capacity. Moreover, the bank was decidedly opposed to passing on the benefits of productivity increases in the form of "wages pushed up arbitrarily . . . by the power of organization. . . ." Because the bank rejected the notion that "workers in a given industry have a prior claim to the benefits resulting from improvements to which they have made no personal contribution"—a policy that would interfere with the "natural distribution of such benefits" as rewards to "those who have been instrumental in accomplishing the improvements"—it proposed instead a policy of lowering prices (National City Bank 1925, 191, 194, 193).

Buffeted both by employers' welfare paternalism programs and open-shop campaigns, AFL membership had fallen by a third from 1920 to 1926 (Wolman 1936, 138). The AFL was therefore reaching for organizing rhetoric that would appeal to employers' self-interest (Phelan 1989, 29–32) by emphasizing that: "When workers realize that increased productivity is the way to . . . higher wages . . ., they are ready for constructive relationships. . . ." Moreover, the Federation urged business not to interpret demands for productivity-linked higher wages "as an attempt to restrict profits. Quite the contrary is true. . . . By assuring an adjustment between consuming power and productivity, the unions are helping to maintain business conditions that make profits possible" (*American Federationist* 1928, 148–49).

This underconsumptionist-accommodationist version of the social wage can, to be sure, plausibly be interpreted as "an affirmation of yearning to increase the efficiency of capitalistic enterprise [that] was ideologically very remote from the thesis of class struggle" and expressed the AFL's need to transcend business and craft unionism (Millis & Montgomery 1945, 172). After all, when Secretary of Labor Davis told the AFL in 1927 that "there is no essential conflict between capital and labor" inasmuch as "[e]ach is dependent on the other, like a general and his army," Green thanked him for seconding the Federation's high wage policy (AFL 1927, 142–43, 150). Moreover, the whole purpose of Frederick Taylor's scientific management movement was purportedly to achieve high wages for workers and low labor cost of manufacture for employers (Taylor 1912a, 22) by inducing both sides to "take their eyes off of the division of the surplus as the all-important matter, and together turn their attention toward increasing the size of the surplus until this surplus becomes so large that it is unnecessary to quarrel over how it shall be divided" (Taylor 1912b, 29–30). The AFL's new wage policy was then expressly welcomed as an admission of the correctness of scientific management (Garrett 1928).

Nevertheless, the suggestion that businessmen regarded the AFL's new productivity-oriented wage policy as "the final triumph of their efforts to steer the philosophy of organized labor into sound economic waters" (McKelvey 1974, 95), is not fully persuasive because it overlooks the fact that the concept of the relative wage furnished unions with a statistical instrument for directly attacking profits in a zero-sum contest over the surplus—the AFL did, after all, see a perfect business cycle correlation between prosperity for firms and depression for workers and vice versa (Kuczynski 1927d).[7] In contrast, bargaining over real wages had that effect only inadverently. Moreover, because the social wage policy did "not intend to keep wages exactly on the same level with prices and productivity" (Green 1927, 924), in principle it permitted rolling back the rate of surplus value cyclically or secularly. Indeed, *American Federationist* published an article in 1927 asking whether some workers might even find productivity-linked wage policy too timid: "Are wages to increase no faster than production increases? Is labor's relative share in the total social income to remain as it is . . .? Is the American Federation of Labor expressing its belief that nothing can be gained by more equitable distribution?" (Gluck 1927, 217). And on the eve of World War II, Green himself was still arguing that "[o]ur policy of productivity wages . . . served to bring to wage earners a larger portion of the increasing wealth they produced" (Green 1939, 100).

It was on precisely such class grounds that the National Industrial Conference Board, a right-wing economic research organization associated with the National Association of Manufacturers (Domhoff 1971, 191), criticized the AFL's new wage policy "as an abstract dictum" which left open the possibility of workers' and unions' laying claim to "all the surplus wealth created. . . ." The Conference Board also expressed skepticism about the AFL's readiness "to modify its traditional policies of restriction of output and control of labor force" (National Industrial Conference Board 1926, 15, 18). It is, therefore, misleading to assert that bankers applauded the AFL's new position because it turned attention away from "struggle for a greater share" (Dorfman 1969, 67).

With the question of "the relation of productivity to wages . . . very near to the hearts of all of us" (Clague 1927, 289), by the time of its 1927 convention, the AFL announced that it had begun publishing studies of the relationship of wages to prices and productivity: "For the first time Labor is exploring the field of government statistics to ascertain whether its share in national income is equitable and whether wages paid to wage earners enable them to share in advances in material civilization" (AFL 1927b, 37). Who or what finally impelled the Federation to embark upon this contentious undertaking?

President Green's Marxist Ventriloquist

The reason that Green's "Modern Wage Policy" Declaration seemed so curiously suggestive of Marx's own popularization of the theory of exploitation is that it was, implausibly enough, written by a German Marxist mole in the AFL.[8] That person, who was also responsible for developing the data on relative wages for the AFL, and thus for the organization's conversion to a crypto-Marxist strategy of holding the line on the rate of surplus value, was twenty-two year-old Jürgen Kuczynski, son of Robert René Kuczynski, perhaps the most eminent economic and demographic statistician in Europe in the first part of the twentieth century (Kuczynski 1957). Born in 1904 into a German-Jewish family with a long intellectual lineage, already as a teenager Kuczynski came into contact with many of Germany's leading intellectual and political figures from Einstein to Kautsky, who formed his parents' intellectual and political circle in Berlin. Robert Kuczynski, whose son was proud of the praise that Lenin had once lavished on his father's book on wages and hours, worked closely with the Communist Party of Germany (KPD), whose "smart leadership could do more with" with such a "high-profile personality" as a non-party-member (Kuczynski 1973, 17–18, 34, 39–41, 78, 107). The elder Kuczynski always remained "true to the Party and to the Soviet Union" and five of his six children became Communists (Kuczynski 1957, 62; Kuczynski 1973, 35).

The younger Kuczynski received his doctorate in 1924 for a dissertation on economic value, over which his father had fallen asleep in the bath tub. Two years later he published his first book; entitled, *Zurück zu Marx (Back to Marx)*, which for the author was synonymous with "forward with Lenin . . . in the conquest of the capitalist world" (Kuczynski 1926d, 145, 167); it was a devout exegesis, which a half-century later the author self-ironically observed he was no longer educated enough to understand (Kuczynski 1973, 52–99). In 1927 he published a comparative study of state finances in capitalist and communist states in which he adopted a primitive vulgar-Bolshevik view of class struggle according to which "the expenditures of the capitalist state serve exclusively the welfare of the ruling class of capitalists." After the class-conscious oppressed class suppressed capitalism by means of a violent revolution, a socialist or communist state arose which was the mirror image of the capitalist state. In 1927 Kuczynski was not speaking theoretically, but meant quite concretely Soviet Russia, which "administers justice for the protection of the interests of the working masses" (Kuczynski 1927c, 32, 40). *Die Internationale,* the journal edited by the Central Committee of the KPD, was quick to acknowledge Kuczynski as a Marxist apprentice who had adopted a class standpoint (R. 1928).

In September 1926, several months before this contribution to Marxist-Communist dogma was published, Kuczynski departed for the United States, where his father, who spent half of each year at the Brookings Institution and as late as 1931 was a member of its advisory council, had secured him a stipend at the short-lived Robert Brookings Graduate School of Economics and Government. Through his father, Kuczynski again came into social contact with many scholarly and political leaders in Washington, D.C., including Justice Brandeis, a distant relative (*Brookings Institution* 1931, 26; Kuczynski 1973, 111–19; Smith 1991, 20–23; Critchlow 1985, 76–81).

Shortly before his departure for the United States, Kuczynski was struck by Paul Douglas's recent article comparing the movements of real wages, production, and productivity. Although Douglas did not draw the parallel or discuss its significance, he presented data showing that from 1899 to 1923, the real earnings of manufacturing wage-earners had risen 28 per cent whereas their per capita output or productivity had increased 52 per cent (Douglas 1926, 33, 42).[9] Kuczynski then published a piece in the *Finanzpolitische Korrespondenz*, which his father edited, in which he methodologically went a step beyond Douglas: by dividing the index of real wages by the index of production, he generated an index of "the share of industrial workers in the total product of industry." This "social standard of living," which Kuczynski conceded was very rough and in need of refinements, had declined by 50 per cent between the turn of the century and World War I and remained stagnant thereafter (Kuczynski 1926a).

In the course of re-reading Douglas on the boat to the United States, a "fundamental idea" dawned on Kuczynski—namely, that the relationship between production and real wages was nothing but Marx's idea of relative wages.[10] Whereas only bourgeois theorists and especially social-democratic revisionists contested Marx's "'theory of absolute immiseration,'" relative immiseration seemed, once the absolute variant was accepted, self-explanatory.[11] The reason that no one had thought of calculating relative wages was the lack of relevant data. When Kuczynski realized on the boat that statistics recently published in the United States had made such calculations possible, he arrived in Washington with his "tongue hanging out" (Kuczynski 1973, 122–25). In November 1926, two months after his arrival, he published two more articles in his father's journal on relative wages, which were both suffused with a primitive version of ameliorative underconsumptionism. In one, expressly referring to Marx's distinction between real and social standards of living, he loosely defined the latter as (wage-working) consumers' share of the national product (Kuczynski 1926b). In the other he presented the first fruits of his calculations of relative wages in several industries as the result of dividing real wages (measured both by a cost of living index and an index of wholesale prices of the particular industry) by productivity (Kuczynski 1926c). In 1927 and 1928 Kuczynski published additional articles on the same subject in Germany until the relative wage "had again found its place as a category of Marxist doctrine" (Kuczynski 1973, 125–26).

While refurbishing Marxism, Kuczynski also performed a much more spectacular feat: ventriloquizing President Green. Although Frey's efforts at the 1925 AFL convention had "given a great movement a great idea," Kuczynski was disappointed that the Federation had "forgotten" about computing the worker's share of the product or implementing the new principle (Kuczynski 1928b, 26). To be sure, Kuczynski overstated his own and underestimated the AFL's initiative: immediately after the Atlantic City convention, *The New York Times* had published an interview with Green in which he anticipated by a year Kuczynski's call for a workers' share index. Specifically, Green stated that the AFL should do research to show workers and the public "how the purchasing power of wages has varied . . . and what relation that curve bears to the output per worker" (Clark 1925, 14).

Kuczynski gained his entrée to the AFL through an acquaintance at Brookings, Margaret Scattergood, who was an assistant to Florence Thorne, secretary to Samuel Gompers, the long-time president of the AFL, and then to his successor, Green. Thorne, who was then organizing a research staff ("Florence Thorne" 1973), gave Kuczynski access to the monthly *American Federationist*, which had already published Frey's article containing thoughts "which, let us say, do not stand all too far from the concept of relative wages" (Kuczynski 1973, 130). Kuczynski's project was also furthered by the accessibility of the BLS, all the commissioners of which (including Carroll Wright, Ethelbert Stewart, Isador Lubin, and Ewan Clague) from its inception in the 1880s until 1965 were friendly with the Kuczynski family. By July 1, 1927, barely nine months after his arrival in the United States, Kuczynski had managed to be appointed the director of the AFL's new statistical department with the special duty of developing relative wage statistics (Kuczynski 1973, 126–36).

Kuczynski's political state of mind as he embarked on his mission at the AFL is nicely captured by family correspondence. On November 7, 1927, Kuczynski wrote to his future wife (in English): "'Ten years Soviet Russia[—]when Soviet Germany!'" Several days later, his father, writing from Moscow, where he was the leader of a German delegation of cultural luminaries to the tenth anniversary celebration of the October Revolution, told his son that "'Soviet Russia *is* the future'" (Kuczynski 1973, 169–71).

Against the background of Kuczynski's strong and visible pro-Marxist, communist, and Soviet sentiments, it is remarkable that in his memoirs he expresses no surprise on that account that the AFL nevertheless hired him. To be sure, his books may have been "completely unknown" in the United States (Kuczynski 1994b), but, despite his age, he had already accumulated a considerable left-wing paper trail that the German trade union movement, with which the AFL maintained friendly relations, could easily have been asked about. Moreover, Green's secretary, Thorne, had a classical education and graduate school social science training that would have made it plausible for her to make such inquiries

(Thorne 1957; "Florence Thorne" 1973). The AFL's robust anti-communism suggests that it must have been concerned about vetting its employees' ideological orientation. In November 1926, for example, even as Kuczynski was publishing articles on relative wages in Germany that would have been completely unacceptable to the AFL, Green, unwittingly anticipating Kuczynski's modus operandi, editorialized that communists "are revolutionaries who use the tactics of intrigue and maneuver" (Green 1926, 1430). And the following October, at the same AFL convention that praised Kuczynski's articles in the *American Federationist* for rendering "a great service," Green, echoing the sentiments of Secretary of Labor James Davis, who lauded the AFL "for keeping out of its ranks men who would try to improve us by Russian or communist methods," reiterated that the Federation "would never have anything to do with Communism or Communistic activity" (AFL 1927b, 289, 145, 193).

Perhaps, as Kuczynski's luck would have it, the AFL did not suspect any connection between Marx and Kuczynski's advocacy of social wages because Kuczynski's fellow student at Brookings, Elsie Gluck, had led the Federation astray by writing in the *American Federationist* that Marx's theory of surplus value was based on the discredited iron law of wages (Gluck 1925, 1164).[12] In any event, in a less bureaucratized world, where personal connections weighed heavily, Kuczynski, who viewed himself "at that time not at all as a communist, but rather as an 'independent Marxist'" (Kuczynski 1994b), was able to occupy the statistical cockpit of the U.S. trade union movement.

Green, "a personally decent, petty-bourgeois compromise figure" amidst "brutal, corrupt" presidents of the individual unions making up the AFL, and Kuczynski, who at the time was writing a book in German about American factory workers which a Soviet reviewer praised as refuting the fairy tale about the capitalist paradise in the United States, made very strange bedfellows indeed (Kuczynski 1973, 137–38, 174–77).[13] Although Green may have shared Kuczynski's experience of never having met a socialist in the AFL, he was surely not asking himself, as was Kuczynski, how one "could carry on class struggle in this country outside of the A.F. of L." (Kuczynski 1973, 183, 141). Kuczynski imagined that his first task at the AFL was not research, but the creation of the basis and program of a relative wage policy as crowned by a wage proclamation to be issued by Green. Kuczynski then wrote the policy which was eventually published in the August 1927 issue of *American Federationist* under Green's name.

Before the arrangement was finalized, however, a problem arose when "an ass from the Federation said that social wages was socialism," causing Green's secretary, Thorne, to become anxious and requiring the parallel publication of an explanatory commentary. In order to get the commentary published, Kuczynski had to use all his guile, charm, and flattery with Thorne and Scattergood. Green, who came to call him "Mr. Jürgen," finally signed, but changed Kuczynski's title, "New Wage Policy," to "Modern Wage Policy," probably, Kuczynski speculated, in order to avoid the public impression of change (Kuczynski 1973, 141–43, 179).

The "sensation" triggered by Green's proclamation may have dumbfounded Thorne, but it delighted Kuczynski, who in his memoirs, published almost a half-century later, offered this account of "the greatest pseudo-success of his life":

> The whole thing was of course nothing but an ideological "coup" [Husarenstreich]: The reactionary president of the A.F. of L. delivers a declaration on wage policy, which breathes more than a breath of genuine Marxist spirit—the declaration said nothing more and nothing less than that the A.F. of L.-union in the future would demand wages that would prevent the increase of exploitation, indeed would reduce it in the course of time. . . . The whole thing really makes the impression of an ideological farce [Posse]. The reactionary A.F. of L. sends a wage declaration out into the world which clearly and distinctly for any theoretically educated Marxist contains the idea of taming capital's craze for exploitation—whereby the declaration had been theoretically and textually worked out in complete isolation by a young postgraduate student. . . . An ideological farce, impossible to perform in a farce theater because it seems so improbable in every respect—except it was in fact reality [Kuczynski 1973, 143–44, 146–47].

Kuczynski's role at the AFL expanded beyond the wage policy. He represented the Federation in various governmental agencies (such as the Bureau of the Census) and non-governmental statistical organizations; on behalf of the AFL he also appeared in public calling for wage increases and shorter hours (Kuczynski 1973, 168; "Asks Higher Wages" 1928). Although Kuczynski ghost-wrote other articles for Green—or, perhaps more accurately, manipulated Green into signing them—the latter's suggestibility was apparently not without limits. Thus after Green had accepted the annual economic preview article that Kuczynski had drafted for 1928, when Kuczynski prognosticated in December 1928 that a continuing decline in relative wages would lead to an economic crisis in 1929, the draft was rejected as too pessimistic (Kuczynski 1973, 165, 177–78).

Looking back from the vantage point of the 1970s, Kuczynski—whose memory, as already noted, was not completely accurate on this point—was also amused that "monopoly capital" had been maneuvered into welcoming this socialist-like policy "'of taming the monopolies'": because its own campaign on behalf of increasing productivity was based on the claim that the results would benefit the whole people rather than merely profit-takers, "the monopolies" were precluded from refuting the

AFL's wage policy. Nevertheless, Kuczynski, in conceding that his coup, of brief effect, "vanished without leaving traces" except for the "very modest" one of the regular publication of relative wage indexes, even with aid of hindsight, overlooked its seminal impact on ULC (Kuczynski 1973, 146–47).

At the end of September 1928, Kuczynski left the full-time employ of the AFL in response to an invitation from the Brookings Institution to write a book on employment statistics. Although Green had complained that the *American Federationist* had become too statistical, he solicited Kuczynski's further (paid) collaboration on the magazine. At the annual convention that year, the Executive Council, without mentioning him by name, listed all of Kuczynski's pamphlets that the AFL had published and singled out the monthly index of the "share employed labor has in the growing opportunity which progressing industry offers" (AFL 1928a, 43). That same year the AFL republished two collections of Kuczynski's *American Federationist* articles. Naming Kuczynski's name, Green welcomed his "vanguard study" of labor's share in value added "or, from the point of view of the manufacturer, . . . the costs of wages to the manufacturer" (AFL 1928b, 6–7), and even recommended the studies to "trade union officials . . . for special use in wage negotiations" (AFL 1928c, 5).

Upon his return to Germany in 1929, Kuczynski, who knew that he would vote for the Communist Party, found the social democratic trade union umbrella organization (Allgemeiner Deutscher Gewerkschaftsbund) too sophisticated to be infiltrated and uninterested in the development of the kinds of statistics he had been able to manipulate the AFL into financing. In 1930 he joined the KPD (Kuczynski 1973, 179, 187, 198),[14] and extended his study of relative wages to Western Europe—research that would eventually mushroom into his postwar 40–volume *History of the Conditions of Workers Under Capitalism* (Kuczynski 1934). Following his sister Ursula, "the famous Soviet spy" (Kuczynski 1994a), Kuczynski became a self-professed Soviet spy in exile. Despite being the head of the KPD in England, he became a lieutenant-colonel in the U.S. Army in England during World War II; assigned to the U.S. Strategic Bombing Survey, he worked with Paul Baran and Paul Sweezy, who became the leading Marxist economists in the United States. After the war, he returned to East Germany, where he became a phenomenally prolific, distinguished, and high-ranking dogmatic Marxist economic statistician and historian with close ties to the leaders of the ruling communist party (Sozialistische Einheitspartei Deutschlands), Walter Ulbricht and Erich Honecker (McElvoy 1990; Williams 1987, 25–28, 34, 48–50; Kuczynski 1973, 286, 399–416; Kuczynski 1992, 18).

Shortly after World War II, Kuczynski, in celebrating the centennial of Marx's development of the concept of relative or proportionate wages—which Marx himself gave Ricardo credit for having fixed as a political-economic category (Marx 1978, 1042)—engaged in self-celebration by stressing that eighty years had passed before he, Kuczynski, undertook the first calculations of relative wages for the AFL. Although he did not inform the AFL in the 1920s that the purpose of collecting relative wage data was to show the class polarization of misery and wealth under capitalism (Kuczynski 1947, 769, 770), in October 1927, Kuczynski inaugurated in the AFL's *American Federationist* "the monthly publication of an index of Labor's share in economic progress," which Green editorially welcomed two months later (Green 1927b). The data showed both the share of wages in manufacturing industry income and labor's "share in the products on the market, which Labor can buy." Both series were merely indexes of trends for the 1920s rather than absolute levels (Kuczynski 1927a, 1232).

At the same time *American Federationist* began publishing a series of more detailed studies on individual industries by Kuczynski (and his wife-to-be, Marguerite Steinfeld, who was simultaneously working at the National Bureau of Economic Research, whose director, Wesley Mitchell, was Robert Kuczynski's long-time friend) (Kuczynski 1973, 130–35). In these micro-studies Kuczynski showed absolute levels and index numbers for wage-earners' share in value added as well as for real income.[15] These data would, Kuczynski assured the membership, enable unions to determine whether labor's share had declined and, if so, whether the decrease had resulted from an increase in salaried workers, the purchase of especially expensive machinery, or "because the profits of owners or stockholders increased very much. . . ." The practical upshot of such investigations was, according to Kuczynski, empirical support for demands for an increase in labor's share where the other groups had garnered "unjustified increases" (Kuczynski 1927b, 1235).

Scattergood, who had made it possible for Kuczynski to work at the AFL, even anticipated his approach: in July and August of 1927 she published two articles in *American Federationist* calculating social wages separately for male and female automobile workers by dividing the cost of living index by an industry-specific productivity index (Scattergood 1927). That same year, the AFL republished Kuczynski's articles as a pamphlet, accompanied by President Green's introduction certifying that they were an "application of the Federation's Modern Wage Policy." Kuczynski, in turn, passing Marx over in silence, testified that the AFL and Green were his inspiration (Kuczynski & Steinfeld 1927a, 5, 7). Kuczynski also emphasized that the new wage policy represented not only a statistical refinement, but also a fundamentally different conception of the production process and of the worker's role in it as well as of the interrelation between production and consumption (Kuczynski & Steinfeld 1927b, 558–59).

Taking his readers behind the methodological curtain, Kuczynski explained how he computed social wages. Merely dividing total wages by the total value of production in manufacturing would be deceptive because the result did not take into account increases in the number of wage-earners and in the population. Correctly conceived, the numerator (wages) had to be divided by the number of wage-earners, while the denominator (production) had to be divided by the total population. Parallel to this social wage index, Kuczynski constructed a series showing "the cost of wages to the manufacturer." A kind of proto-ULC, its denominator included the income of industry with the exception of that spent on raw materials. Unlike the social wage index, which had fluctuated considerably between 1899 and 1925 and had risen a total of 18 per cent, the relative cost of wages had moved within a very narrow band (Kuczynski & Steinfeld 1928, 830–35).

Significantly, Kuczynski saw no relationship between the movements of real wages or social wages on the one hand and those of the cost of wages on the other: wage increases would therefore not necessarily raise the relative cost of wages to employers. This interpretation was presumably designed as a selling point to employers, to whom Kuczynski was apparently suggesting that increasing social wages would not only save them from overproduction crises but also leave their costs unaffected. The underdeveloped state of ULC was highlighted by the fact that although the AFL was clear that "productivity is . . . not an element separate from costs, but enters into the calculation of costs, including labor costs" (*American Federationist* 1928, 148), Kuczynski himself mentioned productivity as an afterthought, observing that other factors such as management, salesmanship, and productivity had a greater influence in reducing the burden or compensating for wage increases (Kuczynski & Steinfeld 1928, 835).

In his memoirs, Kuczynski asserted that the fact that neither the "Declaration" nor the accompanying "Comments" had referred to Frey's earlier statements about the relationship between wages and productivity had given them a "fundamental" character and made them newsworthier. Yet the press failed to understand the social and ideological significance of the "Declaration"—namely, that it would bring about "at a minimum, a halt to the intensification of exploitation." Neither Green nor the presidents of the individual AFL unions caught on either, although the latter protested Green's unilateral promulgation of the declaration without having consulted with them. Why readers failed to grasp Kuczynski's sly Marxist point is unclear since the "Comments" omitted mention of the one scenario (productivity increases in excess of wage increases) under which the rate of surplus value would rise—"Wages may keep pace with prices and productivity, wages may increase more, wages may decrease less" (Green 1927, 924). In any event, in order to defend Green and his own new research department, Kuczynski had to argue that the policy merely synthesized earlier statements by Frey and other union leaders. What "confused" the situation even more, according to Kuczynski, was that at the time he had—in order to protect the new wage policy against attacks by the AFL's antisocialist leadership—to insist that the policy "had nothing to do with socialism," because even if it had been implemented, which would have been objectively impossible, it would merely have checked the expansion and deepening of exploitation but would in no way have "oriented [policy] towards its abolition" (Kuczynski 1973, 145–46).

The left's reaction to Kuczynski's efforts was largely opportunistic. The Labor Bureau Inc.'s economic newsletter hailed the index as a "praiseworthy experiment in a new field" although it raised questions as to whether productivity should be computed macro-or microeconomically ("Labor's Share in Production" 1927).[16] German Social Democracy welcomed the AFL's conception of the social wage as a belated demand by a nonsocialist labor movement for the social equality of classes, which, the AFL would eventually be compelled to recognize, was incompatible with capitalism. Fritz Tarnow, a German trade union leader, observed— in a piece Kuczynski himself found "exceedingly interesting" (Kuczynski 1973, 143)—somewhat condescendingly that what underlay Green's notion of the social wage was the struggle against "relative immiseration."[17] Social democrats applauded a policy that enabled the working class to overcome capitalism without committing economic suicide by succumbing to that "hopelessly pessimistic" doctrine of relative immiseration. Writing in the newspaper of the German counterpart to the AFL, Tarnow gently criticized Green for his exaggerated claim of novelty. What the new policy, which was common to European unions as well, embodied was the insight that the greatest spur to higher wages was not so much the struggle between capital and labor for a larger share but the larger social product made possible by increasing productivity (Tarnow 1927).

Despite the fact that a fellow-traveller had been instrumental in introducing into U.S. wage contests an explicit measure of the results of class income distribution struggles, Marxist-Leninists were contemptuous of mere relative immiseration, which they considered an insipid revisionist plot to divert attention from full-blooded absolute immiseration, which was the proletariat's universal fate (David 1971, 55–59; A. Enderle et al. 1973, 59–60). Soviet Marxists, bound by the Stalinist denunciation of social democracy in all its manifestations as social fascism—a policy of which Kuczynski himself approved (Kuczynski 1973, 202–203)—derided Green's notion of the social wage. On the one hand, a social wage policy merely accommodated capitalists' (self-contradictory) hopes of mitigating underconsumption crises; on the other, it also fit comfortably within capitalist ideology by eliminating surplus value from the distribution struggle: by limiting wage demands to productivity-created additional value, social wage theory focused merely on reducing the value of constant capital embodied in machines and materials in favor of variable capital (i.e. wages) (Kriwizki 1929, 395–405). Despite this predictable propagandistic onslaught, Kuczynski later reported that within days of the first publication of his relative wage index in *American Federationist* in 1927 a "Soviet-Information-Man" in Washington had told him that he had immediately forwarded the index to Russia with the comment that it was "the first original thing that the A.F. of L." had done (Kuczynski 1973, 159–60).

American Marxism also ridiculed the AFL's new wage policy. Lewis Corey, for example, who had spent 1929 at the Institute of Economics at Brookings after having left the Communist Party USA (Draper 1966, 293–302), citing a study done by Kuczynski after his return to Germany, expressly linked exploitation and relative wages by making the decline in relative wages a "characteristic of capitalist production" in general: "Relative wages . . . fall continuously. The fall is usually greatest when the productivity of labor rises most rapidly. [I]n 1929, relative wages fell to the lowest point in American history in the midst of an extraordinary rise in the productivity of labor, surplus value, and profits." Corey, who by this time had developed an ambiguous relationship to the Party, also regarded social wage policy as hopelessly naive because it ignored the "irreconcilable" "fundamental antagonism between profits and wages" (Corey 1934, 82–83, 92). But then even an orthodox economist and Federal Reserve Bank official could agree that: "The great difficulty about raising wages as a means of raising national income is the conflict between wages as income and wages as cost" (Williams 1945, 369).

The criticism offered by William Z. Foster, a leader of the CPUSA and its chief labor spokesperson, lacked the Soviets' or Corey's theoretical or empirical sophistication. For Foster the new wage policy was

> simply [a] fancy name[] for surrendering the trade unions entirely to the greedy exploitation of the capitalists in return for the right of the bureaucrats to collect dues from the workers. The workers had but to work faster and faster and then, by some hocus-pocus, which the A.F. of L. leaders never explained, they would automatically and without struggle, get higher wages. . . .

But beneath the mounds of invective against the AFL's "lackey-like" complicity in "this reactionary speed-up program" lay a glimmer of recognition that in the right proletarian hands, this "platonic argument in favor of higher wages" (Foster 1937, 189, 190; Foster 1947, 100) might bear progressive fruit. This opportunistic attitude is corroborated by Kuczynski's memoirs, which showed sympathy for the "hard time" that Foster was having in the Communist Party in 1927 and 1928. And although Kuczynski criticized the Party for its failure to recognize the propagandistic possibilities opened up by relative wage data for pillorying exploitation, he also proudly reported that when his sister Ursula came to the United States in 1928 and transferred her membership from the German to the American Communist Party, the latter expressed its appreciation for Kuczynski's work in the AFL and took over the computation of relative wages after he left the United States. By the same token, Kuczynski retrospectively justified his own failure to join the CPUSA in 1927–28 on the ground of its unsound (Lovestoneite) leadership and by virtue of the fact that it would have been "unhealthful" for a young person to start his Party career as an illegal member—a step that his work for the AFL would have made necessary (Kuczynski 1973, 181, 144–45, 180, 156–57).

In one of the articles he wrote in 1928 for *Finanzpolitische Korrespondenz* and republished as a book while still in Washington—and which the KPD's *Die Internationale* praised as contributing to the destruction of the legend of the "American workers' paradise" (Lenz 1928)—Kuczynski warned his German audience that the AFL's new wage policy represented neither a conversion to socialism nor a struggle against "relative immiseration." For although Green's "Declaration" could be interpreted to mean that the workers should receive an increasing share of production, it was certain that it would "never" be so interpreted by the AFL. Instead, the AFL's goal was merely to insure that that share did not fall—an objective diametrically opposed to "all socialist principles" and consistent with its acceptance of the status quo. Concealing his role and understating his own hopes for the policy, Kuczynski argued that the Federation had come to recognize the possibility of preventing the rapid immiseration of the masses because it strove to cooperate with business and could induce workers to participate in productivity-enhancing programs only if they too benefited from them (Kuczynski 1928b, 28). Two years later Kuczynski conceded that the notion that wages should rise in tandem with total output was connected with Marx's idea that because wages do not so rise workers must immiserate relatively: "But . . . the A.F. of L. never knew that one could produce the slightest connection between its wage theory and Marx's theory of immiseration." He seemed resigned to the fact that the AFL had adopted the position of a "dignified burgher" who wanted to make sure that no one took anything of his but who also had no intention of seeking revenge for the relative immiseration of previous decades (Kuczynski & Kuczynski 1930, 169–70).

Kuczynski himself went on to make a career not of preaching the efficacy of the social wage as trade union policy, but of using the relative wage as a readily available statistical magnitude reflecting the rate of surplus value. Characterizing relative wages as "an expression of the aggregate societal relationship between working class and capitalists" and "a function of the fundamental antagonism between capital and labor," he argued that it must decline from one business cycle to the next (Kuczynski 1968, 102). In this spirit, he devoted a considerable part of the rest of his life to trying to show the continuous rise in the rate of exploitation in numerous countries and in the world at large (Kuczynski 1967, 125–27). After his departure from the United States, Kuczynski's legacy fell to the CPUSA, which through the Labor Research Association periodically updated his relative wage calculations (Kuczynski 1973, 180; Labor Research Association 1947, 53–55; Labor Research Association 1949, 43–44).[18]

"A Conspiracy So Immense"[19]

The national state was itself no stranger to the collection of data on productivity, output, and wages. As early as the 1890s, Congress had authorized the U.S. Commissioner of Labor to conduct extensive detailed investigations of the effects of the displacement of hand by machine labor on wages (U.S. Commissioner of Labor 1899). By the mid-1920s, against the background of what the BLS deemed "a new industrial revolution . . . perhaps the most remarkable advance in productive efficiency in the history of the modern industrial system" ("Index of Productivity" 1926, 1), Kuczynski's friend Ewan Clague (Kuczynski 1973, 129), whose public prediction in 1933 that "the economic future of this country is to be state socialism" would delay his reconfirmation as Commissioner of Labor Statistics two decades later (U.S. Senate 1955), inaugurated publication of data on industrial productivity in the Bureau's *Monthly Labor Review.* Although "the problem of the distribution of the gains [lay] entirely outside the scope" of the series ("Index of Productivity" 1926, 19), the BLS observed that alone from 1919 to 1925, productivity in manufacturing had risen by one-third ("Comparison of Employment" 1927; "Productivity of Labor" 1927). Matching real wage data with the newly released productivity series, Soule's economic newsletter immediately announced that productivity was outstripping wages ("New Light on Productivity" 1926).

At the outset of the Depression of the 1930s, the U.S. Commissioner of Labor Statistics carried Kuczynski's work farther back in time. Shortly after the AFL's Atlantic City convention, Frey met Ethelbert Stewart, who "good naturedly" asked why the Federation had adopted its new wage policy and "'ruined much of the work which I have done for a lifetime. . . . Now you have done something which destroys the value of cost of living statistics. Now I will be compelled to begin to gather information concerning man's increasing power to produce'" (AFL 1927b, 195). Stewart, another Kuczynski family friend, soon reproduced census data on manufacturing showing "the relative share of wage earners in the product of their labor" from 1849 to 1929. In current dollars Stewart computed the share of wages—in absolute terms and as an index—both in the value of the products produced and in value added. Both the former ratio, approximating a symmetrical ULC (SULC), and the latter ratio, the wage-share, exhibited a steady decline over the whole period. Although Stewart's article also purported to be a study of "the relation between the purchasing power of the wages paid to labor and the value of the products of that labor," he failed to create a series of real wages based on price movements (Stewart 1930).

The depression that seemed to result from the relentless decline in ULC during the 1920s furnished the opportunity for developing the empirical data for refining the concept of ULC. The social crisis of unemployment and the fear that labor-saving innovations would preclude the possibility of the eventual reemployment of the unprecedented mass of unemployed spurred the Works Progress Administration (WPA) to undertake a National Research Project on *Reemployment Opportunities and Recent Changes in Industrial Techniques* directed by David Weintraub. Shortly before the advent of the New Deal, Weintraub had published an article on technological unemployment during the 1920s in which he developed a novel unit labor cost index (Weintraub 1932, 386).[20] One of Weintraub's WPA studies, *Production, Employment and Productivity in 59 Manufacturing Industries, 1919–36,* generated the kind of data on output and productivity that were required for calculating reliable ULC. Congress motivated its funding of this project in 1939 by reference to the two million workers who had been disemployed by labor-saving devices during the previous decade:

> Statistics pertaining to productivity and labor costs are necessary in efforts to prevent technological unemployment. These statistics will show in what industries work hours should be shortened where new machinery and techniques have increased productivity and reduced labor costs.
> Figures are also needed by employers and employees for wage negotiations. By making adjustments in those industries where scientific advance

makes shorter hours and higher wages possible, the problem of technological unemployment can be attacked at its source and controlled through the normal channel of trade-union agreements [U.S. House of Representatives 1939, 1–2].

The principal author to whom the National Research Project entrusted this pro-labor and pro-union study was a recently graduated statistician, Harry Magdoff, who had been knocking on doors in search of a civil service job in Washington. Magdoff worked as a statistician for several federal agencies during the New Deal and World War II, rising in 1946 to special assistant to the Secretary of Commerce, Henry Wallace (U.S. Civil Service Commission 1943, 60; 1944, 61; 1945, 233; 1946, 178; U.S. Senate 1953, 286–326; Hillard 1985, 397–98; Magdoff 1994). For this work he was later credited with having designed the method of measuring production and productivity that the BLS still uses today and that underlies ULC calculations (*Biographical Dictionary of Marxism* 1986, 207). While engaged in that government work, Magdoff, who unlike many later researchers, conceded that there was "no 'true' measure of productivity or production for a group of diverse products," observed that "[t]he problem with which we were confronted arose from an already existing allocation of human and natural resources which was determined through the operation of the market" (Magdoff 1939, 317–18).

McCarthyites later charged that under Weintraub, who had "occupied a unique position in setting up the structure of Communist penetration of governmental agencies," the National Research Project "appears to have been a kind of trap door, through which agents of the Communist underground gained entrance to the Government." A naturalized U.S. citizen from Central Europe, Weintraub, unlike many other victims, answered all of the Senate Judiciary Committee's questions. He denied ever having been a Communist and expressed disbelief that Magdoff or others whose names had been named were Communists. His admission that he had been a member of the Young Socialist League, however, elicited no further questions (U.S. Senate 1952, 4627–80, 4719–37). As a reward for full disclosure and cooperation, Weintraub was forced to resign from a high-ranking position at the United Nations in 1953 ("11 in U.N." 1953; Hamilton 1953).

Among the alleged Communists whom the Project had "harbored" was Magdoff (U.S. Senate 1953b, 10), with whom Weintraub had written an important empirical article in 1940 on the shift to service employment, which also subtly dealt with the concomitant phenomena of proletarianization (Weintraub & Magdoff 1940). In 1948, the "self-styled espionage-exposer and professional witness" (Navasky 1982, xxiii n.) Elizabeth Bentley apostrophically accused Magdoff before the House Un-American

Activities Committee (HUAC) of being part of the "Perlo group" of federal employees engaged in espionage on behalf of the Soviet Union—a charge of which the FBI had allegedly been aware since 1945 (U.S. House of Representatives 1948, 685, 687, 691–92; U.S. Senate 1953b, 1–2). Five years later, Magdoff, one of whose federal supervisors surmised that he read Russian because his parents had been born in Russia, endured similar accusations in person before the Senate Subcommittee to Investigate the Administration of the Internal Security Act, which added the allegation that he had already been a communist in college. Refusing to name names (including Perlo's), Magdoff, who by this time in the progress of McCarthyism had been relegated to self-employment (U.S. Senate 1953a, 286), availed himself of the Fifth Amendment—or, as *The New York Times* headline put it, joined the ranks of those who "Refuse to Tell If They Are Spies" (Trussel 1953).[21]

Magdoff's anti-communist tormentors were so fixated on knowing whether he had betrayed his country by passing on to the Soviet Union secret information on U.S. monthly production of bearings that they totally overlooked his role in the even more insidious surplus value-ULC conspiracy. His more unbalanced congressional persecutors even threw him into the same communist pot with the Ford Foundation and the *Encyclopedia of the Social Sciences*. After working as a stockbroker, financial analyst for an insurance company, and insurance salesman, he became a world-renowned expositor of the Marxist-Leninist theory of imperialism and editor of the Marxist socialist *Monthly Review* (U.S. Senate 1953a, 286–326; U.S. Congress 1953, 10,021; Hillard 1985, 398; Magdoff 1969).[22]

As military production and war supplanted the Depression, the U.S. government became increasingly interested in the physical and financial dimensions of labor requirements for rearmament (Clague 1968, 115–16). One of the first government statisticians to work up Magdoff's output data in combination with BLS payroll data in order to generate ULC data—which had exhibited a decline of one-third during the interwar period—was Victor Perlo (Perlo and Bowden 1940).[23] At the time, Perlo, who eventually became chief of the statistics branch of the Office of Price Administration and an economic analyst in the Division of Monetary Research of the Treasury Department with wide ranging responsibilities for foreign trade, worked in the Industrial Economics Division of the U.S. Department of Commerce (U.S.Civil Service Commission 1942, 26; U.S. Senate 1953a, 402–403, 442–43).

In between federal government jobs, which lasted from 1933 to 1937 and again from 1939 to 1947, Perlo worked at the Brookings Institution at the request of his former boss at the Home Owners Loan Corporation, Spurgeon Bell (U.S. Senate 1953a, 389). At Brookings—where he met

Kuczynski, who was again sojourning in the United States, this time collecting money for the KPD (Perlo 1994; Kuczynski 1973, 306–10)— he became general assistant to Bell, the author of one part of a series of studies constituting "a general re-examination . . . of the operation of the capitalistic system of wealth production and distribution." Perlo was responsible both for developing much of the statistical basis of the study which made unit wage cost a linchpin of the relationships among productivity, wages, and national income, and preparing the chapter on ULC and RULC, both of which showed a sharp decline during the 1920s and 1930s. Because he returned to the federal government before the project was completed, he was not responsible for its interpretations or conclusions (Bell 1940, vii, 3, 44–55). The conclusions that Bell, who eventually became president of a mutual fund trading in commodity futures ("Spurgeon Bell" 1968), reached would presumably have been uncongenial to Perlo. In particular, Bell's claim that gains to labor from increased productivity were realized "chiefly in the form of greater leisure" (Bell 1940, 176) must have seemed sheer mockery during a period of catastrophic unemployment. Equally unpalatable to Perlo must have been Bell's proposal, rooted in pre-Keynesian orthodoxy, that productivity increases be distributed in the form of lower prices rather than as higher wages (Bell 1940, 174–84). Bell's wage-price policy recommendation was identical to the approach adopted by the president of the Brookings Institution, Harold Moulton, who, in addition, deemed redistribution of income from rich to poor useless and that of wealth impracticable (Moulton 1935, 72–83, 117–27; Moulton 1936, 12–18). Instead, "the essence of the good society as Moulton saw it [was] class reciprocity, an equal exchange of benefits from one class to the other" (Smith 1991, 124).

Several months after the ULC article that Perlo co-authored had appeared, his co-author from the BLS published a more detailed account of wages and productivity in the *Monthly Labor Review* in 1940. The BLS's interest in this area was galvanized by the changes in the labor market brought about by the introduction of federal wage and hour and labor relations legislation during the 1930s. Basing itself in part on the framework developed by the Perlo-Bell Brookings study, this new article proved to be unusual if not unique in focusing on (the decline in) RULC and labor's share (Bowden 1940, 517, 520–21, 528, 528 n.8, 540–44). A series of BLS follow-up reports during World War II did not return to these issues ("Labor Productivity" 1941; "Productivity and Unit Labor Cost" 1942; "Productivity and Unit Labor Cost" 1943; Gody & Searle 1946, 914–16). Indeed, the BLS appears to have lost interest in ULC for the next fifteen years; by the time it returned to the subject in 1960, inflation had ousted class income distribution as the whole point of ULC data.

Before then, however, Perlo took his turn jousting with Richard Nixon and other demagogues before the auto-da-fé. In 1948 Bentley, the "red spy queen" (Packer 1962, 52–120), testified before HUAC that Perlo had been the head of a group of federal employees passing secret data through her to Stalin. Indeed, she asserted that Perlo had once literally asked her: "Is Joe getting all this stuff safely?" When Perlo refused to name names (including Magdoff's), *The New York Times* named his on its front page, complementing it with a large photograph on an inside page (U.S. House of Representatives 1948, 677–701; Trussel 1948; U.S. Senate 1953a, 425). Whittaker Chambers weighed in with similar accusations against Perlo (Chambers 1952, 345–46). Five years later Perlo, who, like Magdoff, had in the meantime been thrust down into the ranks of self-employed economic consultants, was also required to appear before the Senate Subcommittee on Internal Security. He again invoked the Fifth Amendment in refusing to answer questions about Magdoff and others (U.S. Senate 1953a, 384–85). As with Magdoff, the congressional anti-communists' obsession with Perlo's access to data on struts and turrets blinded it to what he had helped pass on to the United States from Communism—to wit, class-conscious ULC.

Attacks on Perlo did not end at the highpoint of anti-communist witch hunts in 1953, but continued into the 1960s (U.S. Congress 1958, 18461–71; U.S. Congress 1960, 8431). His unvarnished criticism of U.S. capitalism and imperialism in the 1950s appears to have made him a bête noire of the McCarthyites, who were incensed that: "The man who wielded this power in the Government of the United States is now an open propagandist for the Soviet world conspiracy" (U.S. Senate 1953b, 32). In 1954, as Perlo was publishing an update of Kuczynski's relative wage data in order to prove that the rate of exploitation had increased since the end of World War II (Perlo 1954, 53–56), Representative Gwinn included Perlo among the "dozen individuals loyal to Moscow, [who had] dictated policies of the United States in important and vital particulars." Indeed: "Benedict Arnold was a patriot compared to . . . Victor Perlo" (U.S. Congress 1954, 4849). In 1956, he was accused of having instructed a communist National Labor Relations Board examiner in the 1940s to decide a case against the workers in order to foment dissatisfaction against their employers (U.S. House 1956, 3335; U.S. House 1955, 3004). Ten years after he had left the employ of the federal government, members of Congress were still blaming Perlo for the allegedly Marxist inspiration of U.S. free trade policies (U.S. Congress 55, 5562; U.S. Congress 1957, 3015–16). Perlo, who eventually became the chief economist and a member of the central committee of the Communist Party USA, did not return to the ULC controversy until the 1970s (U.S. House of Representatives

1948, 677–701; Contemporary Authors 1981, 524; *Who's Who in American Jewry* 1980, 370).

From Proletarian Struggle Against Surplus Value Extraction to Capitalist Wage-Push Inflation-Fighting

The category of asymmetrical ULC (AULC) or nominal ULC (NULC) (Rebitzer 1988, 393) is used by economists for two distinct but related purposes. On the one hand, ULC, together with unit nonlabor costs and unit profits, which all add up to total unit costs, form the basis for constructing price deflators and hence price indexes. The unit cost approach is thus a statistical reflection of that Smithian tradition within economic theory (Smith 1937, 48–54) that regards price determination as "the sum of the returns to the factors of production" (Schultze & Tryon 1960, 5). Adding up the wages, profits-interest, and rent paid out by the firm/economy reveals, according to this so-called Trinitarian Formula, how prices are formed (Marx 1964, ch. 1, 48–51). At the same time, however, the widely held belief among economists that inflation accelerates when the increase in labor costs exceeds that in productivity is rooted in the hypothesis that firms set prices as a mark-up above productivity-adjusted labor costs (Mehra 1990, 31): "Since labor cost is a substantial portion of total cost in manufacturing, changes in labor cost are frequently associated with changes in industrial prices" (Chandler & Jackman 1965, 1067).[24] A measure of real (constant dollar) output as the denominator of the unit cost expressions derives from the need for a non-price influenced element against which the inflationary movements of the components can be gauged. Because a productivity or real output measure is needed on the price/cost side, a real or symmetrical ULC (RULC or SULC) that expressed both compensation and output in current or real terms would be inappropriate inasmuch as symmetrical ULC would conceal the contribution of the various price components to inflation.

On the other hand, ULC is also used in descriptive and normative analyses of income distribution between labor and capital. In this context, however, AULC—compensation in current dollars divided by constant output—fails to provide the appropriate basis for dealing with distributional issues. Since one of the functions of ULC is to to educate the public about wage-price-productivity relationships (Solow 1966) and to make transparent the extent to which labor is able to capture productivity increments by securing wage rate increases in excess of the latter (Kendrick & Sato 1963), the use of current rather than real wage data is inappropriate. First, the way in which real output increases resulting from rising productivity are distributed between labor and capital is not directly visible if labor's share appears in inflated form; such a procedure necessarily exaggerates the share of wages and salaries in national income.[25] This methodological bias is not evident on its face because BLS data for output and compensation per man-hour are published in the form of indices. If these series were calculated in dollar terms, their asymmetrical construction would become obvious at the point at which hourly compensation exceeds hourly output.

Second, both economists (Kendrick & Sato 1963, 978–79) and the BLS (Mark 1975; Mark & Kahn 1965) recognize the need for RULC data "to compare real compensation per man-hour and productivity" in order to determine "whether there has been a shift in the distribution of income between factors of production" (Mark & Herman 1970, 32). And third, precisely "[i]n order to provide meaningful information on whether labor has shared proportionately in the gains in labor productivity" (Alterman 1971, 25) or how real wages in a particular industry or firm have developed in relation to economy-wide productivity increases for purposes of collective bargaining (Backman 1954, 65), the BLS itself publishes the requisite real compensation per man-hour data in its ULC tables—yet it has failed to use them to calculate RULC (BLS 1974, 183–84).[26]

In spite of RULC's usefulness in understanding income distribution over the long run as well as during phases of the business cycle,[27] economists (Hultgren 1960; Moore 1983, 245–80), journalists, and government officials have traditionally based their analyses and policy recommendations on AULC.[28] To cite but one of many such press reports: A.H. Raskin of *The New York Times*, for years "America's foremost labor reporter" (Chamberlain 743), stated in an article on collective bargaining prospects that union demands for catch-up wage increases to compensate for inflation had "run into increasingly assertive demands by industry that any increases in labor costs must be balanced by abolition of restrictive work rules and other measures to increase productivity." Raskin saw "stiff employer resistance" as "keyed to worries about the fragile recovery and inflation's squeeze on profit potentialities. . . ." As implicit supporting material, a chart, titled, "Wage Gains Far Outstrip Productivity," was appended to the article. Taken from the BLS's ULC data, it showed that for the years 1971 to 1975, hourly compensation increased more than six times as much as hourly output (39.4 per cent and 6.5 per cent respectively). Raskin, who was lauded as "especially searching when writing about inflation" (Severo 1993), failed to explain that the data are asymmetrical although he noted elsewhere in the article that real wages had stagnated during these five years.[29] Moreover, the fact that he formulated union claims so as to leave their validity an open question might even lead readers to view the steeply rising wage curve as a corrective for such claims (Raskin 1976).[30] In fact, however, if profitability deteriorated during the first half of the 1970s (Weisskopf 1979, 349; Bowles, Gordon, & Weisskopf 1986, 136), that decline was not caused by immoderate real wage increases, since real compensation per hour lagged behind real output per hour in the private sector (U.S. BLS 1989, 348–49).

Non-Marxist economists' preference for working with nominal magnitudes such as NULC rather than with real income derivatives such as RULC may be a product of the Keynesian revolution in economic thinking and policy.[31] Keynes broke with orthodoxy not only concerning the sufficiency of wage reductions as a means of stimulating recovery, but also with regard to the form of those reductions. Unlike Pigou and other traditionalists, Keynes was convinced that "ordinary experience . . . tells us, beyond doubt, that a situation where labour stipulates (within limits) for a money-wage rather than a real wage . . . is the normal case. Whilst workers will usually resist a reduction of money-wages, it is not their practice to withdraw their labour whenever there is a rise in the price of wage-goods" and "no trade union would dream of striking on every occasion of a rise in the cost of living" (Keynes 1967, 9, 15). Consequently:

> [A] movement by employers to revise money-wage bargains downward will be much more strongly resisted than a gradual and automatic lowering of real wages as a result of rising prices. [W]hile a flexible wage policy and flexible money policy come, analytically, to the same thing, inasmuch as they are alternative means of changing the quantity of money in terms of wage-units, in other respects there is . . . a world of difference between them [Keynes 1967, 264, 267].

Among these differences, Keynes noted that capitalist societies lacked a mechanism for decreeing uniform across-the-board wage reductions. The means that were available for reducing money wages involved "a series of gradual, irregular changes, justifiable on no criterion of social justice or economic expediency, and probably completed only after wasteful and disastrous struggles, where those in the weakest bargaining positions will suffer relatively to the rest." But what a "flexible wage policy" could not achieve, an inflationary money policy could: "A change in the quantity of money . . . is already within the power of most governments. . . ." Under these circumstances, Keynes concluded, "only . . . a foolish person . . . would prefer a flexible wage policy to a flexible money policy" (Keynes 1967, 267–68).

To be sure, such indirect methods of shifting income from mass consumption to investment did not originate with Keynes, who merely conceptualized already existing practices, which included the levying of indirect taxes (Luxemburg 1923, 374–75). A senior research advisor in the International Monetary Fund outlined the short-run benefits that Keynes perceived in such inflationary policies:

> Keynes was very clear that the constructive influence was a profit inflation rather than an income inflation—allowing prices to rise by more than wages, so that businessmen pocketed the difference. . . . Inflation then leads to forced saving by consumers, who allow their real income to be reduced by the increased prices they pay to entrepreneurs [Hirsch 1969, 137].

The latter part of the Eisenhower administration, marked by a moderate resurgence of nonwar-induced inflation (U.S. Bureau of the Census 1975, 210), was a prime example of how "[t]he subject of unit . . . labor costs, at one time aroused sporadic interest, which tended to be highly correlated with the occurrence, or the threat of inflation" (Greenberg & Mark 1968, 105). By 1958 the Committee for Economic Development (CED), a research and policy planning instrument of big business (Domhoff 1971, 123–24, 189–94), issued a report stating that "the main problem is in the field of labor, where there is no law and not even a public philosophy or policy for the limitation of economic power," and urging consideration of legislation to curb unions' power (CED 1958, 16). The CED concurred in the policy recommendation advocated by American Keynesians a decade earlier that wages should rise in proportion to—that is, that labor and capital should share in—economy-wide productivity increases "without encroaching unduly upon the profit margin" (Hansen 1945, 259; Hansen 1947, 244–45; Hansen 1951, 573). Unlike the British Keynesian Joan Robinson, however, the CED was not so sanguine as to believe that: "The main defence against the tendency to stagnation comes from pressure by trade unions to raise money-wages. . . . If . . . real wages can be made to rise as fast as output per man the root of the trouble is cut . . . " (Robinson 1971, 94).

This policy of linking wage increases to macroeconomic productivity increases had been incorporated into the collective bargaining agreement between General Motors and the United Automobile Workers in 1948; the next year, the President's Council of Economic Advisers (CEA) became an advocate of the policy, albeit in non-programmatic fashion (Bortz 1948; U.S. Council 1949, 45). In light of the Marxist connection to social or relative wage theory and the central role that rising productivity occupies in Marx's theory of capital accumulation and crisis (Marx 1867, 599–699), it is ironic that the founder of end-of-ideology ideology asserted in the 1950s that the advent of productivity-linked annual wage increases—indeed, the relatively new idea of productivity itself—constituted a refutation of Marx's analysis of capitalism, which saw wealth as secured through "'exploitation'" (Bell 1966, 220). For unlike many laborite, leftist, and even communist authors, who forged a Ricardian underconsumptionist program that focused exclusively on relative wages or surplus value as subject to a voluntaristic struggle between labor and capital in the sphere of distribution (Glyn & Sutcliffe 1972),[32] Marx argued that crises are ushered in by periods in which labor's share rises (Marx 1963, 409) and that "the wealth of society and the possibility of the constant expansion of its process of reproduction depends not on the length of the surplus labor, but rather on its productivity . . . " (Marx 1964, 828). Moreover, Marx centered his theory of accumulation on the self-contradictory process of self-valorization of capital. Only this complex dynamic incorporating the relationship between living and dead labor (the organic composition of capital) and the rate of exploitation was, in Marx's view, adequate to conceptualize the cyclical and secular movements of the rate of profit and their effects on class struggle (Altvater et al. 1974; Schmiede 1973).

To buttress its position on wage increases, the CED argued that the distribution of all after-tax corporate profits as wages "would clearly have disastrous effects on productivity, production and employment. Moreover, the stability of labor's share suggests that feasible action in a free market is unlikely to change the share materially." From the claim that an investment strike by capital demonstrates the futility of expropriation (Backman & Gainsbrugh 1949, 194) this non sequitur was supposed to follow: "Therefore, it is a reasonable conclusion that, for labor as a whole, real income cannot rise faster than real output" (CED 1958, 15, 56–57). In order to provide the requisite empirical underpinnings for its agenda, the CED immediately commissioned a study of unit costs by Charles Schultze as a contribution to analysis of the question as to whether inflation was inevitably associated with low unemployment (Schultze 1959, 4 [no pagination]). As a result of excellent timing and the CED's membership links to influential public opinion-shaping media organizations, the CED's position was popularized (Collins 1981, 142–44) and "quickly swept into the main flood of national debate" (Schriftgiesser 1967, 82).

Despite the world industrial hegemony that the United States still exercised, by 1960 the BLS regarded manufacturing ULC as part of the answer to the question as to "how to restore the kind of total balance of payments that will enable the United States to finance a desirable level of foreign aid" (Arnow 1960, 693). Because "hourly labor cost in U.S. industry is much higher than in any other country, frequently two to four times that of the countries of northern Europe and even higher in relation to Italy and Japan," economists began asking whether the outflow of gold, increased U.S. investment abroad, and increased imports of manufactures reflected differences in labor cost between U.S. and foreign firms (Shelton & Chandler 1963b, 485; Goldberg & Moye 1985, 204). Thus during the half-decade following the Korean War, U.S. imports of finished manufactures rose by 133 per cent whereas exports increased by only 25 per cent; during the same period, 1954–1959, U.S. direct investment in manufacturing in Western Europe doubled (U.S. Bureau of the Census 1975, 889, 870).

Economists and policy makers also focused on labor costs because they were "the primary cost factor of production," "can be controlled to some extent by the addition of capital equipment," and directly affect the well-being of individuals." Since differentials in labor productivity in some U.S. industries exceeded those in wages, firms were able to remain competitive in terms of ULC. This "revival of interest in cost—especially labor cost—comparisons . . . stimulated" the BLS to develop ULC data (Shelton & Chandler 1963b, 485–86, 488–90) both domestically and internationally (Chandler & Jackman 1964; U.S. BLS 1966).

In 1962 the CEA began making elaborate use of ULC data for the purpose of establishing "guideposts for noninflationary wage and price behavior" within the framework of an incomes policy (U.S. Council 1962, 167–90; U.S. Council 1967, 119–34; U.S. Bureau of Economic Analysis 39–40; Sheahan 1967). Taking as its "point of departure" a constant distribution of income between labor and capital, President Kennedy's Council at the height of Cold War put the "arithmetical relationships among output per man-hour (productivity), wage rates, and prices" (U.S. Council 1967, 120) in their global context:

> It is no accident that productivity is the central guidepost for wage settlements. Ultimately, it is rising output per man hour which must yield the ingredients of a rising standard of living. Growth in productivity makes it possible for real wages and real profits to rise side by side.
>
> Rising productivity is the foundation of the country's leadership of the free world, enabling it to earn in world competition the means to discharge its commitments overseas [U.S. Council 1962, 190].

Borrowing the wage guideline "out of the CED book almost word for word" (Schriftgiesser 1967, 89), the Council ascribed a pivotal position to the development of ULC insofar as it regarded a stable price level as dependent on a macroeconomically strictly parallel growth rate between compensation per hour and output per hour. If prices then moved in accordance with ULC, "the relative shares of wages and returns to capital will remain constant" (U.S. Council 1968, 122). To these propositions the CEA later added that "since the capital employed per unit of output shows little trend in most sectors, the rate of return on capital will remain stable" (U.S. Council 1968, 122).[33] This set of propositions, which the Council regarded as a realistic description of basic economic processes, was then supported by ULC data for several branches. From them the CEA concluded that "when wages rise faster than output per man-hour, prices rise correspondingly with little effect on the distribution of income" (U.S. Council 1968, 122–23). Startlingly enough, this policy of setting wages and prices in accordance with changes in macroeconomic productivity appears to have been first proposed by Kuczynski himself (Kuczynski & Kuczynski 1930, 161–66).

The Council thus implied on the one hand that firms are generally able to pass on wage costs (in the form of higher prices) in order to protect the rate of return on their capital. On the other hand, the Council overlooked the fact that mere constancy of factor shares must lead to further inequalities in the distribution of income if the share of wage and salary workers in the total labor force is on the rise. In other words, official data on labor's share of national income are overstated because they do not take into account the fact that workers become an increasingly larger proportion of income recipients as the proportion of capital-income recipients declines (Millis & Montgomery 1938, 56–57; Uhlmann & Huber 1971, 112–37; Adam 1973; Skiba & Adam 1974, 89–114; U.S. Council 1967, 132).[34]

From this analysis it is evident that despite the Council's admission that "there is nothing immutable in fact or in justice about the distribution of the total product between labor and nonlabor incomes" (U.S. Council 1962, 186), its identification of price stability with constant ULC constituted a plea for acceptance of the existing division of income between labor and capital. Yet even this defense of the distributional status quo demonstrated that the growth and consolidation of unionization during the intervening half-century had doubtless contributed to the sea change that had evolved since Frederick Taylor had enunciated the microeconomic principle that when an innovation increased workers' productivity four-fold, raising their wages by more than 60 per cent made "many of them . . . work irregularly and tend to become more or less shiftless, extravagant, and dissipated. [I]n other words . . . it does not do for most men to get rich too fast" (Taylor 1911, 74).

The Council's plea was nevertheless ironic in light of the fact that the period during which the "guideposts" were formulated was marked by declining ULC and labor's declining share in total output (U.S. Council 1967, 85; U.S. Council 1974, 73). Consequently, U.S. manufacturing firms' ULC position vis-à-vis foreign competitors improved significantly: in a trend reversal of the previous half-decade, the growth of U.S. exports of finished manufactures exceeded that of imports by 53 per cent to 42 per cent between 1959 and 1964 (Chandler & Jackman 1965; U.S. Bureau of the Census 1975, 889). This development, which included a slowing of the growth rate of real hourly compensation in manufacturing by one-third so that RULC declined 3.8 per cent after having risen 2.8 per cent from 1954 to 1959 (Mark & Kahn 1965, tab. 2 at 1058), favored the strong cyclical accumulation of capital that took place during the first half of the 1960s.

That the CEA nevertheless avoided open espousal of a policy of accumulation-via-declining labor shares lay only partly in ideology; for the optimism generated by the then longest postwar boom influenced the articulation of economic policy. It is therefore conceivable that the Council, extrapolating from this experience, concluded that high growth rates could be achieved with stable prices and without business cycles if labor and capital shared equally in future productivity increases and if the latter were high and matched by those in capital intensity (U.S. Council 1967, 133; Perlo 1973, 26). However, the accumulation and profit boom, which had in part been fed by low ULC in the first half of the 1960s—from 1960 to 1966 undistributed corporate after-tax profits rose 120 per cent while the after-tax rate of profit for manufacturing corporations rose 46 per cent—brought about a decline in unemployment to its lowest postwar level and an accompanying rise in wages, ULC, and labor's share in national income in the latter half of the decade (U.S. Council 1975, 335, 337, 278–79; Mark & Ziegler 1967, 28–29; Mark & Herman 1970, 32; U.S. Bureau of Economic Analysis, 1984, ser. 64 at 145).

The CEA's fixation on resisting labor's encroachment on capital even misled it from arithmetic to non sequitur: "The disparity between the large nominal gains in hourly compensation and the very moderate increase in real compensation per man-hour in 1966 emphasizes again the fact that more cannot be taken out of the economy than is produced" (U.S. Council 1967, 96). A standard labor economics and labor relations textbook elaborated this capital-logic by asserting "that if labor were to attempt to appropriate for itself the entire increase in labor-hour output, there would be little point in investing additional capital in business" (Bloom & Northrup 1981, 441). Walter Heller, who as chairman of President Kennedy's CEA had formulated the wage-price guideposts, asserted two decades later that employers who could not raise their prices in tandem with wages would "go out of business" (Heller 1980, 88). And President Reagan's CEA repeated the admonition that wages "cannot consistently outstrip productivity growth without diminishing incentives for investment" (U.S. Council 1988, 69).

Andrew Shonfield, the chairman of the British Social Science Research Council and a thoroughly mainstream economist,[35] astutely criticized these ideological constructs, which also flourished in Western Europe:[36]

What the fashionable exponents of "incomes policy" seemed constantly to ignore was that they were asking wage-earners to accept that the existing division of wealth and the income derived from it was basically fair. Their concern, they insisted, was only to agree about the way in which the annual *increment* of national production—after all, a very small percentage of what was already possessed—was to be distributed. Perhaps the optimism arose out of the conviction, which had become widespread by the early 1960s, that economic growth could now be taken for granted: with the secure prospect of an annual bonanza to be shared out, it was argued, why should people quarrel about it? . . . [W]hat is implied by arguments derived from theoretical economics about the proper remuneration of factors is the acceptance of a large block of the *status quo.* Labour is really being asked to give its consent to a particular type of social order. There is no reason why it should willingly do so . . . [Shonfield 1969, 217–19].

The CEA sought to defend itself against such charges. Thus despite its declaration that the guideposts merely "suggest a proportionate sharing of average national productivity gains among labor, capital, and the other related factors of production," the Council asserted that their purpose was not "permanently to freeze the labor and nonlabor shares": "it is consistent with the guideposts for wage and profit shares to be bid up or down in a particular industry so long as price behavior in that industry is consistent with the general price guidepost . . ." (U.S. Council 1964, 119–20). Robert Solow, who had worked with the Council during the early 1960s, tried to come to its aid by repeating the CED's argument: the critics' complaint about freezing functional income distribution "has no practical weight at all" because that division between labor and property changes very slowly and within a narrow range.[37] Since "there is every reason to believe that market forces will never, or hardly ever, want to move the proportional distribution of income very rapidly" the guideposts give "all the room needed for the market to operate" (Solow 1966, 48–49).

When the recession phase of the cycle reasserted itself in 1969–70 and ushered in an extended period of stagflation, which Keynesian fiscal policies proved incapable of mastering, state pressure to prevent the rising wage rates that would interfere with accumulation reassumed its accustomed role—this time in the form of a Keynesian "income policy that would check the rise of unit labour costs" (Phelps Brown 1983, 162–63). During these years the so-called wage-price spiral controversy shaped economic policy formation worldwide (Blechschmidt 1974). In July 1971, Arthur Burns, the chairman of the Board of Governors of the Federal Reserve System, testifying before Congress that "labor seems to have become more insistent, more vigorous, and more confident in pursuing its demands, while resistance of businessmen to these demands appears to have weakened" in part because public welfare programs "can be called upon to help sustain a striking employee," urged government wage-price action (Burns 1971, 661–62). The so-called wage-price freeze that was implemented in the United States in August 1971 was a version of the incomes policies that Western European countries had already developed (Weber 1973; Flanagan, Soskice, & Ulman 1983, 1–22). These less subtle Keynesian wage-cutting policies were designed to strengthen employers' position by "curb[ing] money wage rates in relation to prices" and creating a "lower real wage rate per unit of labor. . ." (Smith 1968, 116).

The reformed social contract that is reputedly the prerequisite of any incomes policy designed "as an instrument to achieve . . . real wage reductions [through] asymmetrical restraint in wages and prices" (Flanagan, Soskice, & Ulman 1983, 10) is, however, particularly difficult to forge in the early recovery phase and the late prosperity phase of the business cycle. It was, therefore, not fortuitous that at the same time the Nixon administration revealed plans to relax price controls in order to "ease profit margins" in 1973, the business press demanded a continuance of the wage freeze in order not to undermine the incipient upswing. Although economists conceded that "a freeze that continues for any significant time does place a burden on labor since the increased productivity of labor leads to higher profits rather than higher wages" (Bosworth 1972, 353), the federal government was so appalled by opinion polling that showed that "nearly 85 per cent of all union members think stockholders rather than employees are the major beneficiaries of productivity gains" that it induced the Advertising Council to grant it $10 million of space and time "to overcome this kind of misunderstanding"—which 20 per cent of executives shared (*Monthly Labor Review* 1972, 2).

Even when, as in the 1970s, the real rate of return on manufacturing and corporate capital in the United States did decline, the increase in real wages was so "modest" that economists have contended that only a nominal, neutral, anti–inflationary incomes policy was called for as opposed to the "real policies" that were openly applied "with the aim of restraining real wages and bolstering profitability" (Flanagan, Soskice, & Ulman 1983, 7,10, 22; Sachs 1979, 278). By the early 1970s, then, it could be said, by a slight modification of the CEA's propositions, that "[s]imple arithmetic requires" (U.S. Council 1968, 122) that, *ceteris paribus*, capital's share rise at labor's expense if nominal rather than real compensation is compared with real output.

What Goes Around Comes Around: The Renaissance of Communist Party Interest in ULC

After having lost the battle against the capitalist defanging and re-colonization of the category of ULC, Soviet and U.S. Communist Party economists in the 1970s resumed the struggle on their enemies' own terrain just as employers embarked on an unprecedented worldwide campaign to curtail increases in ULC. The leading Soviet writer on the U.S. economy, Stanislav Menshikov, for example, contended that "the movement of the unit labour cost is the hub of the most acute social conflicts" (Menshikov 1975a, 260).[38] Accepting the orthodox reasoning associated with ULC, Menshikov assumed a framework within which nominal wage increases equaled cost of living increases times productivity increases; consequently, labor's share in national income had to remain constant. Of such a wage policy Menshikov said that the ratio between the growth rate of total money wages (W) and that of real national income (X):

> reflects the change in the unit labour cost. From the point of view of entrepreneurs, every increase of this cost . . . leads to a decrease in the share of profit and "compels" them to raise prices. From the position of the working class, however, an increase in the unit labour cost is *necessary* if prices rise because otherwise a reduction in its share in the national income is inevitable [Menshikov 1975a, 259–60].

If labor's share is defined as total wages/national income (W/Y) or total real wages/real national income (W_r/X), then wage increases equivalent to price increases times productivity increases must leave labor's share unaffected. Although ULC is directly dependent on price movements, under the assumption of a real-relative wage policy, price rises serve only to increase ULC since workers are automatically compensated for them.[39] Even outside the framework of such a wage policy, the claim that "wage increases in excess of productivity increases are inflationary . . . is true only if there are no shifts favorable to wage earners in the distribution of real income" (Rees 1959, 34).

Under a real-relative wage policy, changes in W/X (ULC) track those in W/Y (SULC) and W_r/X (RULC). From the viewpoint of a hypothetically isolated national capital (Fichte 1845), it would arguably be irrelevant whether ULC rose: under the assumptions of a real-relative wage policy, real wages would not be reduced by price increases and the division of income between labor and capital would remain unchanged. The only requirement would be the absence of any limits on price rises.

Such a requirement would, however, be unacceptable in real-world economies. First, such a national capital would be disadvantaged on the world market since its commodities would carry higher prices than those of national capitals not burdened by the aforementioned mechanism (Flanagan, Soskice, & Ulman 1983, 6). Second, even within a national capital, productivity and thus price level changes vary from industry to industry.[40] If the increase in productivity in certain industries or firms exceeds that of other industries or firms, it is to the former's advantage that their workers receive wage increases equal to the economy-wide rather than the industry-specific productivity increase since that wage policy will result, *ceteris paribus*, in lower ULC and higher profits (Sloan 1965, 399). And third, if the restrictive assumption that wages rise parallel to increases in prices and productivity is dropped, firms' interest in reducing ULC becomes manifest since a lower ULC would be tantamount to a higher total social rate of exploitation.

Writing in the mid-1970s, Menshikov stated that ULC had not fallen in the United States since the recession of 1949. This diminution in cyclical sensitivity he attributed to the greater strength of organized labor, whose long-term collective bargaining agreements blunt the immediate impact of unemployment (Menshikov 1975a, 260–63). This trend toward the conversion of wages from a variable into a fixed cost is exaggerated by Menshikov's use of ULC for the entire economy including the state sector; for ULC have continued to decline cyclically in manufacturing and to a lesser extent in the private sector as a whole. AULC declined in manufacturing in 1950, 1955, 1959, 1962–65, 1983–84, 1987, and in the entire business sector in 1950, 1955, 1963, and 1993 (U.S. BLS 1989, 350). These waves confirm the aforementioned cyclical character of ULC, in particular its association with improved conditions of profitability during the early periods of the recovery phase of the business cycle (*Business Conditions Digest* 1970, 28; *Business Conditions Digest* 1976, 30; *Business Conditions Digest* 1990, 28).

Real wage rate increases, however, lagged considerably behind productivity increases in manufacturing during the post-World War II period. From 1947 to 1993, real hourly compensation rose 112 per cent while constant dollar output per hour increased 256 per cent (see Figure 2, p. 43); (U.S. BLS 1989, 348–50; *Monthly Labor Review* 1994, tab. 44 at 93). For the total business sector, the corresponding figures were 139 per cent and 171 per cent respectively (U.S. Council 1994, 322; *Monthly Labor Review* 1994, tab. 44 at 93). Consequently, during these forty-six years RULC declined 40 per cent in manufacturing (see Figure 1, p. 2) and 12 per cent in the business sector. This across-the-board secular decrease occurred despite the fact that the data on hourly compensation are overinclusive, encompassing not only wages and salaries of employees plus employers' contributions for social insurance and private benefit plans, but also estimates of wages, salaries, and supplemental payments for proprietors and unpaid family workers (U.S. BLS 1989, 353 nn. 2–3).[41]

With nominal compensation rising more than thirteen-fold, NULC, by contrast, quadrupled in manufacturing and sextupled in the business sector (U.S. BLS 1989, 348–50; *Monthly Labor Review* 1994, tab. 44 at 93; U.S. Council 1994, 322). Even the compensation of employees as a

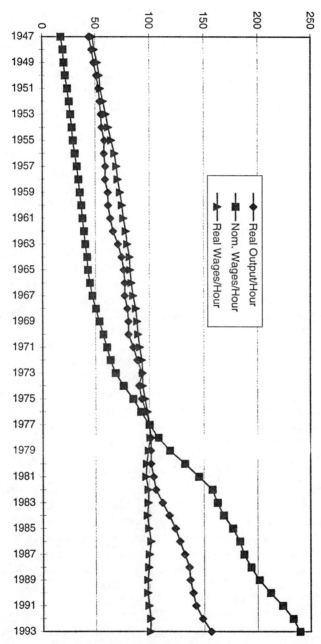

Figure 2: Real Output, Nominal Wages, & Real
Wages in Manufacturing, 1947-93 (1977=100)

share of national income, which, because its numerator includes considerable income that should be classified as profit, is a much less precise
category than RULC in manufacturing, has exhibited a clearly cyclical
trend, declining during all recovery periods (U.S. Bureau of Economic
Analysis 1984, 145; *Business Conditions Digest* 1989, 102). Despite this
tethering of real wages to productivity (Mitchell 1980, 38–39; U.S. Council 1992, 95), economists conclude from the fact that AULC has risen in
most years since World War II that "the notion that wages should advance
only in accordance with increases in productivity is more an intellectual
exercise for economists than a practical reality at the bargaining table"
(Bloom & Northrup 1981, 441).

Three decades after his original contributions to ULC methodology
as a government economist, Victor Perlo of the CPUSA also returned to
the fray, this time openly joining the issues of ULC and surplus value:
"certain types of statistics play a role in the class struggle" and in particular "falsified" ULC data "have become a major weapon of capital" (Perlo
1988, 61–62, 68).[42] Harking back to the underconsumptionist notions that
overtly-covertly underlay the AFL-Kuczynski framework, in the 1970s
Perlo characterized the exploitation-rooted contradiction between production and consumption as the main contradiction within capitalism. After
calculating the high rate of surplus value—"which all employers know,
but they do not speak about it"—as the inverse of labor's share in manufacturing, Perlo shifted to an alternative procedure to take into account
"the effects of monopoly pricing and promonopoly taxation. . . ." Like
Kuczynski almost a half-century earlier, Perlo compared "the physical
volume of the worker's production with the volume of his consuming
power after allowing for changing retail prices and tax deductions. . . ."[43]
Based on the greater availability of data—to which Perlo and Magdoff
had signally contributed—Perlo was able to generate more refined results
than Kuczynski. Perlo accomplished this result "technically by comparing
productivity per . . . man-hour with real take-home pay . . . per man-
hour." In other words, Perlo returned to ULC. To illustrate the defini-
tionally inverse relation between the rate of surplus value and RULC and/
or labor's share, Perlo instanced a 20-per cent increase in productivity
and a 10-per cent rise in real wages: the rate of exploitation (120/110)
rises 9.1 per cent while labor's share (110/120) declines 8.3 per cent. In
an accompanying graph, Perlo plotted a gentle rise in NULC ("Wages
per Unit of Factory Production") and an "almost continuous" decline in
RULC/labor' share after World War II ("Real Take-Home Pay per Unit
of Factory Production") (Perlo 1973, 26–31, 228–29).

In calculating this RULC index, Perlo, like Soviet economists (Vygodskii 1969, 214), strove for greater realism by using the BLS's real
spendable earnings series, which—unlike ULC compensation data, which

include even the employer's share of the social security tax (Alterman 1971, 25)—reflected quasi-take-home pay by deducting federal income and social security (but not state and local) taxes. Perlo justified this methodology on the ground that: "Taxation has become another channel for the realization of surplus value. An increasing portion of taxes is taken from workers and spent for the benefit of capitalists" (Perlo 1973, 26–33). Perlo's use of even realer RULC was part of his and the Communist Party's struggle against "rigged and grossly misleading" government ULC data "designed to assist the antilabor propaganda of big business" that sought to blame inflation on wage increases. Interestingly, in disqualifying official ULC data in part because they include non-surplus value producing sectors, Perlo specifically mentioned "service" industries as "largely irrelevant to the main labor-management struggles over wages (Perlo 1973, 32, 108).[44] This judgment would presumably come as a surprise to the fastest growing and most innovative and confrontational union in the United States, the Service Employees International Union (Ybarra 1994).

By the time Perlo updated and revamped his realer RULC data in the late 1980s, he was no longer able to use the real spendable earnings series. By that time the BLS under the Reagan administration had discontinued it in 1982 "obviously to cover up part of the deterioration in workers' conditions" (Perlo 1988, 59).[45]

In what may have been the final international Communist Party debate over RULC and surplus value, Perlo and Menshikov engaged in a pointed polemical exchange in the wake of the dissolution of the socialist economies of Eastern Europe. In a critique appearing in the last issue of the Prague-based *World Marxist Review* in mid-1990—and published simultaneously in the theoretical journal of the CPUSA (*Political Affairs*)—Perlo took Menshikov to task for having argued at an international round table on "Modern Capitalism" that capitalism had become viable because the bourgeoisie in the advanced industrial nations had siphoned off some of its neocolonialist superprofits to the working class, which had also "managed to secure real wage increases commensurate with higher labour productivity," thus expanding markets and substantially modifying "the tendency toward absolute and relative impoverishment of workers." During the post-World War II period, real wages fell "only during periods of structural crises," whereas declines in labor's share of national income were "more common . . . but . . . not felt so strongly" (Menshikov 1989, 56). Perlo, charging that Menshikov had downplayed the exploitation of wage labor in the advanced capitalist world, contrasted the latter's claims with data showing that the rate of surplus value in the United States had risen and relative wages[46] had declined during the post-World War II period (Perlo 1990a; Perlo 1990b). While insisting in rebuttal that, during the long upturn ending in 1973, increases in real wages had kept pace with those in productivity for all U.S. workers if not for manufacturing, Menshikov indirectly conceded Perlo's empirical point for the entire postwar period (Menshikov 1990).

In this welter of numbers, however, neither side elucidated the political risk that had always underlain Kuczynski's original effort to infuse collective bargaining with surplus-value thinking. That danger was the possibility that orienting wage demands toward productivity increases might, instead of achieving its intended effect of raising working-class consciousness about the historical limits of the capitalist mode of production, ultimately promote the long-term stabilization of capitalism by means of a balanced expansion of mass consumption and production calibrated with the aid of state intervention.

Conclusion

If ULC discourse originated in labor's drive to resist exploitation, orthodox economists eventually succeeded in transubstantiating it into a mere measure of inflation (Kendrick & Grossman 1980, ch. 4). Although the zero-sum struggle between labor and capital became acute during the Depression and then again during the immediate postwar years (Mattick 1969; "Productivity" 1946), by the 1950s the political-economic conflict turned quiescent. As if a reflection thereof, economists' discussions lost their edge and became antiseptic until ULC became, in the words of *The New York Times,* no more than an indicator of "whether any wage increase is being offset by a rise in the value of what each worker produces" (Uchitelle 1987). Ultimately, then, ULC furnished the statistical-methodological underpinning for the dogma that "workers who do not produce more cannot be paid more" (Mead 1992, 74).

To the extent that official use of ULC tolerates even oblique insight into underlying social struggles, it is only from the perspective of a fictitious society at large defending itself against covetous workers: "through its impact on unit labor costs, output per hour is an important element in the wage-price relationship because it is an indicator of the extent to which compensation gains can occur without putting pressure on prices or reducing payments to other input factors" (U.S. BLS 1992, 84). Or, as Magdoff noted in a late contribution, the productivity measurements underlying ULC, which he himself had, at the creation, treated skeptically as a "makeshift" or "convenient fiction," had become "a myth . . . to support propaganda for . . . a reduction in real wages" (Magdoff 1982, 359).

That ULC have displaced labor's share in labor-management relations seems only appropriate in the United States where Clark Kerr, a towering figure of industrial relations, characterized "functional shares" as "a rather dated way of looking at distribution . . . a hangover from the classical economists and the Socialists." Shifting the focus from class to individual size distribution of income had, according to Kerr, "the added advantage that it is less likely to lead to a class-conflict approach to income distribution. . . . From the standpoint of social peace, it is better to discuss the share of . . . the bottom 25 percent of income recipients than . . . in terms of . . . labor's share" (Kerr 1977, 127–28). In contrast to this classless pure pluralism and individualism of the United States, in a reformist-pluralist society such as Germany (Müller 1973, 415–16; O'Connor 1986), the annual report of the counterpart to the U.S. President's Council of Economic Advisers regularly includes a table on labor's share (Sachverständigenrat 1977, 81);[47] in a more class-conscious country such as Italy the sub-headline of a four-column front-page article in the leading daily newspaper virtually shouts the annual change in labor's share at readers (*Corriere della Sera* 1972).

Kuczynski, who began it all by trying to infiltrate surplus value into everyday trade-union thinking and politics, was later amused by his "class-struggle-alien naiveté" in believing that he could have promoted political practice on the basis of a theory within the AFL especially since the wage policy had to remain meaningless for AFL politics (Kuczynski 1973, 144, 157). As the C.P.U.S.A's more recent open espousal of the interlocked connections between surplus value and ULC reveals, however, glasnost' alone does not guarantee agitational success either.

REFERENCES

Adam, H. 1973. "Statistische Probleme bei Einkommensvergleichen zwischen Selbständigen und abhängig Beschäftigten." *WSI Mitteilungen* 26 (9):342–47
Alterman, Jack. 1971. "Compensation Per Man-Hour and Take-Home Pay." *Monthly Labor Review* 94 (6):25–34
Altvater, E., et al. 1974. "Vorbemerkung zu: David Yaffe, Die Krise der Kapitalverwertung—eine Kritik der Thesen von Glyn/Sutcliffe." *Probleme des Klassenkampfes* 4 (3):177–86
American Federation of Labor. 1921. *Report of Proceedings of the Forty-First Annual Convention.* Washington, D.C.: Law Reporter Printing
———. 1922. *Report of Proceedings of the Forty-Second Annual Convention.* Washington, D.C.: Law Reporter Printing
———. 1923. *Report of Proceedings of the Forty-Third Annual Convention.* Washington, D.C.: Law Reporter Printing
———. 1925. *Report of Proceedings of the Forty-Fifth Annual Convention.* Washington, D.C.: Law Reporter Printing
———. 1926. *Report of Proceedings of the Forty-Sixth Annual Convention.* Washington, D.C.: Law Reporter Printing
———. 1927a. *Organized Labor's Modern Wage Policy* (Research Series No. 1). Washington, D.C.: American Federation of Labor
———. 1927b. *Report of Proceedings of the Forty-Seventh Annual Convention.* Washington, D.C.: Law Reporter Printing

————. 1928a. *Report of Proceedings of the Forty-Eighth Annual Convention.* Washington, D.C.: Law Reporter Printing

————. 1928b. *Wages and Labor's Share in the Value Added by Manufacture* (Research Series No. 4). Washington, D.C.: American Federation of Labor

————. 1928c. *Wages in Manufacturing Industries: 1899 to 1927* (Research Series No. 6). Washington, D.C.: American Federation of Labor

American Federationist. 1928. 35 (2):148–49

Arnow, Philip. 1960. "Foreign Trade and Collective Bargaining." *Monthly Labor Review* 83 (7):693–99

Aron, Raymond. 1962. *Dix-huit leçons sur la société industrielle.* Paris: Gallimard

Artto, E. 1987. "Relative Total Costs—An Approach to Competitiveness Measurement of Industry." *Management International Review* 27 (2):47–58

"Asks High Standard for American Labor." 1926. *N.Y. Times,* Jan. 11, p. 20, col. 2

"Asks Higher Wage with Five-Day Week." 1928. *N.Y. Times.* July 29, sect. II, p. 12 col. 2

Backman, Jules. 1954. "Wage-Productivity Comparisons." *Industrial and Labor Relations Review* 8 (1):59–67

————, & M. Gainsbrugh. 1949. "Productivity and Living Standards." *Industrial and Labor Relations Review* 2 (2):163–94

Bell, Daniel. 1966 [1958]. "The Capitalism of the Proletariat: A Theory of American Trade Unionism." In *idem, The End of Ideology: On the Exhaustion of Political Ideas in the Fifties* (rev. ed.). New York: Free Press

Bell, Spurgeon. 1940. *Productivity, Wages, and National Income.* Washington, D.C.: Brookings

Bergmann, Joachim, Otto Jacobi, & Walther Müller-Jentsch. 1975. *Gewerkschaften in der Bundesrepublik: Gewerkschaftliche Lohnpolitik zwischen Mitgliederinteressen und ökonomischen Systemzwängen.* Frankfurt am Main: Europäische Verlagsanstalt

Bernstein, Aaron. 1993. "Don't Blame the Slow Job Growth on Labor Costs." *Business Week,* July 12, p. 120

Bernstein, Irving. 1966 [1960]. *The Lean Years: A History of the American Worker 1920–1933.* Baltimore: Penguin

Biographical Dictionary of Marxism. 1986. (Robert Gorman ed.). Westport: Greenwood

Biographical Dictionary of the American Left. 1986. (Bernard Johnpoll & Harvey Klehr ed.). New York: Greenwood

Blechschmidt, Aike. 1974. *Löhne, Preise und Gewinne 1967–1973: Materialien zur "Lohn-Preis-Spirale" und Inflation.* Lampertheim: Kübler

Bloom, Gordon, & Herbert Northrup. 1981. *Economics of Labor Relations* (9th ed.). Homewood: Irwin

Bortz, Nelson. 1948. "Cost-of-Living Wage Clauses and UAW-GM Pact." *Monthly Labor Review* 67 (1):1–7

Bosworth, Barry. 1972. "Phase II: The U.S. Experiment with an Incomes Policy." *Brookings Papers on Economic Activity* 2, 343–83

Bowles, Samuel, David Gordon, & Thomas Weisskopf. 1986. "Power and Profits: The Social Structure of Accumulation and the Profitability of the Postwar U.S. Economy." *Review of Radical Political Economics* 18 (1&2):132–67

The Brookings Institution: Devoted to Public Service Through Research and Education in the Social Sciences. 1931. Washington, D.C.: Brookings

Buchele, Robert, & Jens Christiansen. 1993. "Industrial Relations and Relative Shares in the United States. *Industrial Relations* 32 (1):49–71

Burns, Arthur. 1971. "Statement." *Federal Reserve Bulletin* 57 (8):653–62

Business Conditions Digest. 1970. 10 (1):28

————. 1976. 16 (2):30

————. 1989. 29 (9):102

————. 1990. 30 (3):28

Business Week. 1974. Oct. 26 (advertisement)

Chamberlain, Neil. 1965. *The Labor Sector: An Introduction to Labor in the American Economy.* New York: McGraw-Hill

Chambers, Whittaker. 1952. *Witness.* New York: Random House

Chandler, John, & Patrick Jackman. 1964. "Unit Labor Costs in Eight Countries Since 1950." *Monthly Labor Review* 87 (4):377–84

————. 1965. "Cost Trends in Nine Industrial Nations." *Monthly Labor Review* 88 (9):1064–68

Clague, Ewan. 1927. "Productivity and Wages in the United States." *American Federationist* 34 (3):285–96

————. 1968. *The Bureau of Labor Statistics.* New York: Praeger

Clark, Evans. 1926. "Union Labor Takes New View of Wages." *N.Y. Times,* Oct. 18, sect. X, p. 1, col. 2

Collins, Robert. 1981. *The Business Response to Keynes, 1929–1964.* New York: Columbia University

Committee for Economic Development. 1958. *Policies for Price Stability in a Growing Economy.* New York: Committee for Economic Development

Communist Party, U.S.A. 1970. *The "Productivity" Hoax!—And Auto Workers' Real Needs!* New York: New Outlook

"Comparison of Employment and Productivity in Manufacturing Industries, 1919 to 1925." 1927. *Monthly Labor Review* 24 (5):16–17

Contemporary Authors. 1981. New Revision Series 2. Detroit: Gale

Corey, Lewis. 1934. *The Decline of American Capitalism.* New York: Covici Friede

Corriere della Sera. 1972. Mar. 31, p. 1

Crotty, James, & Leonard Rapping. 1975. "The 1975 Report of the President's Council of Economic Advisors: A Radical Critique." *American Economic Review* 65 (5):791–811

Cullity, John. 1990. "Diminished Unit Labor Cost Pressures: Importance for Methuselah Expansion." In *Analyzing Modern Business Cycles: Essays Honoring Geoffrey H. Moore* 238–48 (Philip Klein ed.). Armonk: Sharpe

David, F. 1971 [1932]. *Der Bankrott des Reformismus: Wandlungen in der Theorie und der Politik der deutschen Gewerkschaften vom Verzicht auf die soziale Revolution zur Preisgabe des Lohnkampfes.* Erlangen: Politladen

Dencik, Peter. 1974. "Solidarisk Lönepolitik som Inkomstpolitik." In *Arbete, Kapital & Stat: Politisk-Ekonomiska Studier i svensk Kapitalism* 191–214 (Peter Dencik & Bengt-Åke Lundvall eds.). Stockholm: Zenit

"Does Hard Work Bring More Pay?" 1923. *Facts for Workers* 1 (4):1–2

Domhoff, G. 1971. *The Higher Circles: The Governing Class in America.* New York: Vintage

Dorfman, Joseph. 1969 [1959]. *The Economic Mind in American Civilization 1918–1933.* Vol. 4. New York: Kelley

Douglas, Paul. 1926. "The Movement of Real Wages and Its Significance." *American Economic Review* 16 (1):17–53 (Supplement)

———. 1930. *Real Wages in the United States 1890–1926.* Boston: Houghton Mifflin

Draper, Theodore. 1966 [1957]. *The Roots of American Communism.* New York: Viking

"11 in U.N. Accused of Communist Ties." 1953. *N.Y. Times,* Jan. 2, p. 1, col. 2

"Employment and Production in Manufacturing Industries, 1919 to 1936." 1939. *Monthly Labor Review* 49 (6):1397–1404

Encyclopedia of the American Left. 1990. (Mari Jo Buhle et al. eds.). New York: Garland

Enderle, A., et al. 1973 [1932]. *Das rote Gewerkschaftsbuch.* Hamburg: Association

Fichte, Johann Gottlieb. 1845 [1800]. *Der geschlossene Handelsstaat.* In *idem, Sämmtliche Werke.* Vol. 3. Berlin: Veit

Flaim, Paul. 1982. "The Spendable Earnings Series: Has It Outlived Its Usefulness?" *Monthly Labor Review* 105 (1):3–9

Flanagan, Robert, David Soskice, & Lloyd Ulman. 1983. *Unionism, Economic Stabilization, and Incomes Policies: European Experience.* Washington, D.C.: Brookings

"Florence Thorne of A.F.L. Is Dead." 1973. *N.Y. Times,* Mar. 17, p. 34, col. 4

Foster, William. 1937. *From Bryan to Stalin.* New York: International

———. 1947 [1927]. *American Trade Unionism: Principles and Organization, Strategy and Tactics: Selected Writings.* New York: International

Frey, John. 1926. "A Sound Basis for Wages." *American Federationist* 33 (1):26–34

Friendly, Henry. 1968. "The Fifth Amendment Tomorrow: The Case for Constitutional Change." *University of Cincinnati Law Review* 37 (4):671–726

Garrett, Garet. 1928. "The American Book of Wonder." *Saturday Evening Post,* 200 (28): 28–181 (Jan. 7)

"George H. Soule, Jr., Dies at 82." 1970. *N.Y. Times,* Apr. 15, p. 43, col. 1

Gluck, Elsie. 1925. "Wage Theories—Yesterday and Today." *American Federationist* 32 (12):1163–66

———. 1927. "The Significance of Labor's Wage Statement." *American Federationist* 34 (2):214–20

Glyn Andrew, & Bob Sutcliffe. 1972. *British Capitalism, Workers and the Profits Squeeze.* Middlesex: Penguin

Gody, Cella, & Allan Searle. 1946. "Productivity Changes Since 1939." *Monthly Labor Review* 63 (6):893–917

Goldberg, Joseph, & William Moye. 1985. *The First Hundred Years of the Bureau of Labor Statistics.* Washington, D.C.: U.S. Government Printing Office (BLS Bulletin 2235)

Green, William. 1936. "Communists." *American Federationist* 33 (12):1430

———. 1927a. "The Modern Wage Policy of the American Federation of Labor." *American Federationist* 34 (8):919–24

———. 1927b. "Our Index of Labor's Share." *American Federationist* 34 (12):1430

———. 1939. *Labor and Democracy.* Princeton: Princeton University

Greenberg, Leon, & Jerome Mark. 1968. "Sector Changes in Unit Labor Costs." In *The Industrial Composition of Income and Product* 105–47 (Studies in Income and Wealth, Vol. 32; John Kendrick ed.). New York: National Bureau of Economic Research

Hamilton, Thomas. 1953. "Weintraub Resigns U.N. Job Under Fire." *N.Y. Times,* Jan. 7, p. 1, col. 2

Hansen, Alvin. 1945. "Stability and Expansion." In *Financing American Prosperity: A Symposium of Economists* 199–265 (Paul Homan and Fritz Machlup eds.). New York: Twentieth Century Fund
———. 1947. *Economic Policy and Full Employment.* New York: McGraw-Hill
———. 1951. *Business Cycles and National Income.* New York: Norton
Heller, Walter. 1980. "Economic Policy for Inflation: Shadow, Substance, and Statistics." In *Reflections of America: Commemorating the Statistical Abstract Centennial* 81–90 (Norman Cousins ed.). Washington, D.C.: U.S. Department of Commerce
Hemberger, Horst, et al. 1968 [1965]. *Imperialismus heute: Der staatsmonopolistische Kapitalismus in Westdeutschland.* [East] Berlin: Dietz
Herman, Shelby, & Lawrence Fulco. 1969."Productivity and Unit Labor Costs in 1968." *Monthly Labor Review* 92 (6):11–15
Hillard, Michael. 1985. "Harry Magdoff and Paul Sweezy: Biographical Notes." In *Rethinking Marxism: Struggles in Marxist Theory: Essays for Harry Magdoff & Paul Sweezy* 397–405 (Stephen Resnick & Richard Wolff eds.). New York: Autonomedia
Hirsch, Fred. 1969. *Money International.* Middlesex: Penguin
Hoffmann, Walther. 1971. "Zur langfristigen Entwicklung der Lohnstückkosten." *Zeitschrift für die gesamte Staatswissenschaft* 127 (4):576–96
Hultgren, Thor. 1960. *Changes in Labor Cost During Cycles in Production and Business.* New York: National Bureau of Economic Research
"Index of Productivity of Labor in the Steel, Automobile, Shoe, and Paper Industries." 1926. *Monthly Labor Review* 23 (1):1–19
Institute of Marxism-Leninism of the C.C., CPSU. [1964]. *The General Council of the First International 1864–1866: The London Conference 1865: Minutes.* Moscow: Foreign Languages
"John P. Frey Dies." 1957. *N.Y. Times,* Nov. 30, p. 21, col. 1
Kaplan, Lawrence. 1958. "Factors Affecting Productivity in the Homebuilding Industry." Dissertation, Columbia University
Kendrick, John, & Elliot Grossman. 1980. *Productivity in the United States: Trends and Cycles.* Baltimore: Johns Hopkins University
———, & Ryuzu Sato. 1963. "Factor Prices, Productivity, and Economic Growth." *American Economic Review* 43 (5):974–1003
Kerr, Clark. 1977 [1957]. "Labor's Income Share and the Labor Movement." In *idem, Labor Markets and Wage Determination: The Balkanization of Labor Markets and Other Essays* 89–128. Berkeley: University of California
Keynes, John Maynard. 1967 [1936]. *The General Theory of Employment, Interest and Money.* London: Macmillan
———. 1979 [1932]. "Notes on Fundamental Terminology." In *The Collected Writings of John Maynard Keynes.* Vol. 29: *The General Theory and After: A Supplement* (Donald Moggridge ed.). London: Macmillan
Kriwizki, M. 1929. "Die Lohntheorie der deutschen Sozialdemokratie." *Unter dem Banner des Marxismus* 3 (3):381–405
Kuczynski, Jürgen. 1926a. "Produktion und Konsum." *Finanzpolitische Korrespondenz* 7 (40/41):1–3 (Nov. 2)
———. 1926b. "Produktion, Produktivität und Löhne in amerikanischen Industrien." *Finanzpolitische Korrespondenz* 7 (44/45):1–3 (Nov. 22)
———. 1926c. "Reallohn und Produktionsvolumen in Amerika." *Finanzpolitische Korrespondenz* 7 (33/34):1–3 (Sept. 4)
———. 1926d. *Zurück zu Marx: Antikritische Studien zur Theorie des Marxismus.* Leipzig: Hirschfeld
———. 1927a. "Economic Statistics: An Index of Labor's Share in Production and in Consumption." *American Federationist* 34 (10):1231–33
———. 1927b. "Labor's Share in Manufacturing Industries." *American Federationist* 34 (10):1233–44
———. 1927c. *Der Staatshaushalt: Ein Beitrag zur Erkenntnis der Struktur des kapitalistischen und des kommunistischen Staates.* Berlin: Laubsche
———. 1927d. "Wages and Business Cycles." *American Federationist* 34 (9):1095–99
———. 1928a. "Economic Statistics: An Index of Labor's Share in Production and in Consumption." *American Federationist* 35 (3):326–28
———. 1928b. *Löhne und Konjunktur in Amerika.* Berlin: Verlag der Finanzpolitischen Korrespondenz
———. 1934. *Die Entwicklung der Lage der Arbeiterschaft in Europa und Amerika 1870–1933: Statistische Studien zur Entwicklung der Reallöhne und Relativlöhne in England, Deutschland, USA, Frankreich und Belgien.* Basel: Philographischer Verlag
———. 1947. "Statistische Methodologie und Geschichte der Relativlöhne in Deutschland: Zum Hundertjahresalter eines marxistischen Begriffs." *Einheit* 2 (8):767–775
———. 1957. *René Kuczynski: Ein fortschrittlicher Wissenschaftler in der ersten Hälfte des 20. Jahrhunderts.* [East] Berlin: Aufbau

————. 1967. *Eine Weltübersicht über die Geschichte der Lage der Arbeiter.* In *idem, Die Geschichte der Lage der Arbeiter unter dem Kapitalismus.* Vol. 37. [East] Berlin: Akademie

————. 1968. *Die Theorie der Lage der Arbeiter.* In *idem, Die Geschichte der Lage der Arbeiter unter dem Kapitalismus.* Vol. 36. [East] Berlin: Akademie-Verlag

————. 1973. *Memoiren: Die Erziehung des J.K. zum Kommunisten und Wissenschaftler.* [East] Berlin: Aufbau

————. 1992. *"Ein linientreuer Dissident": Memoiren 1945–1989* (2nd ed.). Berlin: Aufbau

————. 1994a. Letter to author. Feb. 23

————. 1994b. Letter to author. Mar. 7

————, & Marguerite Kuczynski. 1930. *Der Fabrikarbeiter in der amerikanischen Wirtschaft.* Leipzig: Hirschfeld

————, & Marguerite Steinfeld. 1927a. *Wages and Labor's Share* (Research Series No. 2)

————. 1927b. "Wages in the Pig Iron Industry." *American Federationist* 34 (5):558–61

————. 1928. "Wages in Manufacturing Industries 1899 to 1927." *American Federationist* 35 (7):830–35

"Labor Productivity and Labor Cost, 1939–41." 1941. *Monthly Labor Review* 53 (6):1388–91

Labor Research Association. 1947. *Labor Fact Book 8.* New York: International

————. 1949. *Labor Fact Book 9.* New York: International

————. 1948. *Trends in American Capitalism: Profits and Living Standards.* New York: International

"Labor's Share in Production." 1927. *Facts for Workers* 1 (6):1

Lauck, W. Jett. 1929. *The New Industrial Revolution and Wages.* New York: Funk & Wagnalls

Lenz, J. 1928. Review of Jürgen Kuczynski, *Löhne und Konjunktur in Amerika. Die Internationale* 11 (24):840

Leven, Maurice, Harold Moulton, & Clark Warburton. 1934. *America's Capacity to Consume.* Washington, D.C.: Brookings

Luxemburg, Rosa. 1923 [1913]. *Die Akkumulation des Kapitals,* In *idem, Gesammelte Werke,* Vol. 6. Berlin: Vereinigung Internationaler Verlagsanstalten

Magdoff, Harry. 1939. "The Purpose and Method of Measuring Productivity." *Journal of the American Statistical Association* 34 (6):309–18

————. 1969. *The Age of Imperialism: The Economics of U.S. Foreign Policy.* New York: Monthly Review

————. 1982. "The Economists' New Clothes." *Nation* 234 (12):359–61 (Mar. 27)

————. 1994. Letter to author. Mar. 8

————, & Irving Siegel, & Milton Davis. 1939. *Production, Employment, and Productivity in 59 Manufacturing Industries, 1919–36* (Works Progress Administration, National Research Program on Reemployment Opportunities and Recent Changes in Industrial Techniques: Studies on the Labor Supply, Productivity, and Production, Rep. No. S-1, pt. 1–3)

Malabre, Alfred. 1976. "The Outlook." *Wall Street Journal.* Jan. 19, p. 1, col. 5

Mandel, Ernest. 1971 [1969]. *Die deutsche Wirtschaftskrise: Lehren der Rezession 1966/67.* Frankfurt am Main: Europäische Verlagsanstalt

Mark, Jerome. 1968. "Wage-Price Guidepost Statistics: Problems of Measurement." *Proceedings of the Business and Economic Statistics Section of the American Statistical Association* 123–29

————. 1975. "Productivity and Costs in the Private Economy." *Monthly Labor Review* 98 (6):3–8

————, & Shelby Herman. 1970. "Recent Changes in Productivity and Unit Labor Costs." *Monthly Labor Review* 93 (5):28–32

————, & Elizabeth Kahn. 1965. "Recent Unit Cost Trends in U.S. Manufacturing." *Monthly Labor Review* 88 (9):1056–63

————, & Martin Ziegler. 1967. "Recent Developments in Productivity and Unit Labor Costs." *Monthly Labor Review* 90 (5):26–29

Marx, Karl. 1867. *Das Kapital: Kritik der politischen Ökonomie.* Vol. 1: *Der Produktionsprocess des Kapitals* (reprint 1959). Hamburg: Meissner

————. 1959 [1849]. "Lohnarbeit und Kapital." In Karl Marx [&] Friedrich Engels, *Werke,* 6:397–423. [East] Berlin: Dietz

————. 1963 [1885]. *Das Kapital: Kritik der politischen Ökonomie.* Vol. 2: *Der Zirkulationsprozeß des Kapitals* (Friedrich Engels ed.). In Karl Marx [&] Friedrich Engels, *Werke.* Vol. 24. [East] Berlin: Dietz

————. 1964 [1894]. *Das Kapital: Kritik der politischen Ökonomie.* Vol. 3: *Der Gesamtprozeß der kapitalistischen Produktion* (Friedrich Engels ed.). In Karl Marx [&] Friedrich Engels, *Werke.* Vol. 25. [East] Berlin: Dietz

————. 1965. Letter to Friedrich Engels, June 24, 1865. In Karl Marx [&] Friedrich Engels, *Werke.* Vol. 31. [East] Berlin: Dietz

————. 1978. *Zur Kritik der politischen Ökonomie (Manuskript 1861–1863).* In Karl Marx [&] Friedrich Engels, *Gesamtausgabe (MEGA).* Div. 2, Vol. 3, Pt. 3. [East] Berlin: Dietz

————. 1992 [1865]. "Value, Price and Profit." In Karl Marx [&] Friedrich Engels, *Gesamtausgabe (MEGA).* Div. 1, Vol. 20: 141–86. Berlin: Dietz

Mattick, Paul. 1969 [1936]. *Arbeitslosigkeit und Arbeitslosenbewegung in den USA 1929–1935*. Frankfurt am Main: Neue Kritik
McElvoy, Anne. 1990. "Berlin Ideologist Keeps Faith with the 'Great' Stalin." *Times* (London), Sept. 29 (Nexis)
McKelvey, Jean. 1974 [1952]. *AFL Attitudes Toward Production 1900–1932*. Westport: Greenwood
Mead, Lawrence. 1992. *The New Politics of Poverty: The Nonworking Poor in America*. New York: Basic
Mehra, Yash. 1990. "Real Output and Unit Labor Costs as Predictors of Inflation." *Federal Reserve Bank of Richmond Economic Review* 76 (4):31–39
Menshikov, S[tanislav]. 1975a. *The Economic Cycle: Postwar Developments* (Leo Lempert tr.). Moscow: Progress
———. 1975b. "How to Treat 'Stagflation.'" *N.Y. Times*, Jan. 5, sect. III, p. 26
———. 1989. "Why Is Capitalism Viable?" *World Marxist Review* 32 (11):54–57 (Nov.)
———. 1990. "Pearls of Dogmatism." *World Marxist Review* 33 (5–6):82–83 (May-June)
Millis, Harry, & Royal Montgomery. 1938. *Labor's Progress and Some Basic Labor Problems*. New York: McGraw-Hill
———. 1945. *Organized Labor*. New York: McGraw-Hill
Mills, Frederick. 1932. *Economic Tendencies in the United States: Aspects of Pre-War and Post-War Changes*. New York: National Bureau of Economic Research
Mitchell, David. 1980. *Unions, Wages, and Inflation*. Washington, D.C.: Brookings
Mitchell, Wesley. 1941 [1913]. *Business Cycles and Their Causes*. Berkeley: University of California
Monthly Labor Review. 1972. 95 (12):2
———. 1994. 117 (3):93
Moore, Geoffrey. 1955. "Business Cycles and the Labor Market." *Monthly Labor Review* 78 (3):288–92
———. 1980. "Inflation and Statistics." In *Contemporary Economic Problems* 167–91 (William Fellner prog. dir.)
———. 1983. *Business Cycles, Inflation and Forecasting* (2d ed.). Cambridge: Ballinger
Moulton, Harold. 1935. *Income and Economic Progress*. Washington, D.C.: Brookings
———. 1936. *Income Distribution under Capitalism: A Challenge to American Business Men*. Washington, D.C.: Brookings
Müller, Wolfgang. 1973. "Der Pluralismus—die Staatstheorie des Reformismus." In *Klassenjustiz und Pluralismus: Festschrift für Ernst Fraenkel zum 75. Geburtstag* 395–424 (Günther Doeker & Winfried Steffani eds.). Hamburg: Hoffmann & Campe
National City Bank of New York. 1925. "A New Labor Declaration." In *Economic Conditions*, 191–95, Nov.
National Commission on Employment and Unemployment Statistics. 1979. *Counting the Labor Force*. Washington, D.C.: U.S. Government Printing Office
National Industrial Conference Board. 1926. *Wages in the United States*. New York: National Industrial Conference Board
Navasky, Victor. 1982 [1980]. *Naming Names*. Middlesex: Penguin
"New Light on Productivity." 1926. *Facts for Workers* 4 (12):2
"New Wage Theory Outlined by Green." 1926. *N.Y. Times*, Feb. 27, p. 5, col. 2
Newman, Barry. 1975. "The Marx-Men: Radical Economists See Slump as a Chance to Popularize Views." *Wall Street Journal*. Feb. 5, p. 1. col. 1
O'Connor, James. 1986 [1984]. *Accumulation Crisis*. Oxford: Blackwell
Packer, Herbert. 1962. *Ex-Communist Witnesses: Four Studies in Fact Finding*. Stanford: Stanford University
Perlo, Victor. 1954. *The Income 'Revolution'*. New York: International
———. 1962. "The Revised Index of Industrial Production." *American Economic Review* 52 (3):496–513
———. 1973. *The Unstable Economy: Booms and Recessions in the United States Since 1945*. New York: International
———. 1988. *Super Profits and Crises: Modern U.S. Capitalism*. New York: International
———. 1990a. "Dangerous Illusions." 33 *World Marxist Review* 33 (5–6):80–82 (May-June)
———. 1990b. "Dangerous Illusions About Capitalism." *Political Affairs* 59 (6):22–26 (June)
———. 1994. Telephone interview with author. Mar. 19
———, & Witt Bowden. 1940. "Unit Labor Cost in Manufacturing Industries, 1919 to 1939." *Monthly Labor Review* 51 (1):33–37
Perry, George. 1972. "Real Spendable Weekly Earnings." *Brookings Papers on Economic Activity* 3, 779–87
Phelan, Craig. 1989. *William Green: Biography of a Labor Leader*. Albany: SUNY
Phelps Brown, Henry. 1968. *A Century of Pay: The Course of Pay and Production in France, Germany, Sweden, the United Kingdom, and the United States of America, 1860–1960*. London: Macmillan
———. 1983. *The Origins of Trade Union Power*. Oxford: Oxford University Press
"Productivity and Unit Labor Cost in Manufacturing Industries." 1942. *Monthly Labor Review* 54 (5):1071–72

"Productivity and Unit Labor Cost in Selected Manufacturing Industries, 1939–42." 1943. *Monthly Labor Review* 56 (5):885–87

"Productivity of Labor in Manufacturing Industries, 1919 to 1925." 1927. *Monthly Labor Review* 24 (6):52–54

"Productivity: The Basic Issue." 1946. *Business Week*, Jan. 19, pp. 86–93

R., G. 1928. Review of Jürgen Kuczynski, *Der Staatshaushalt. Die Internationale* 11 (2):64

Raskin, A. 1976. "Labor Goal Portends Strikes." *New York Times*, Jan. 4, sect. III, p. 60, col. 1

Rebitzer, James. 1988. "Unemployment, Labor Relations, and Unit Labor Costs." *American Economic Review* 78 (2):389–94

Rees, Albert. 1959. "Patterns of Wages, Prices, and Productivity." In *Wages, Prices, Profits, and Productivity* 11–35. New York: American Assembly

Reynolds, Lloyd. 1949. *Labor Economics and Labor Relations.* New York: Prentice-Hall

Robinson, Joan. 1972. *The Accumulation of Capital* (3rd ed.). London: Macmillan

Sachs, Jeffrey. 1979. "Wages, Profits, and Macroeconomic Adjustment: A Comparative Study." *Brookings Papers on Economic Activity* 2, 269–319

Sachverständigenrat zur Begutachtung der gesamtwirtschaftlichen Entwicklung. 1972. *Gleicher Rang für den Geldwert: Jahresgutachten 1972/73.* Stuttgart: Kohlhammer

———. 1977. *Mehr Wachstum Mehr Beschäftigung: Jahresgutachten 1977/78.* Stuttgart: Kohlhammer

"Says Labor Enters New Pay Fight Era." 1927. *N.Y. Times*, July 31, p. 25, col. 1

Scattergood, Margaret. 1927. "Wages in the Automobile Industry." *American Federationist* 34 (7, 8):818–23, 966–71

Schmiede, Rudi. 1973. *Grundprobleme der Marx'schen Akkumulations-und Krisentheorie.* Frankfurt am Main: Athenäum

Schriftgiesser, Karl. 1967. *Business and Public Policy: The Role of the Committee for Economic Development: 1942–1967.* Englewood Cliffs: Prentice-Hall

Schultze, Charles. 1959. *Prices, Costs and Output for the Post War Decade: 1947–1957.* New York: Committee for Economic Development

———, & Joseph Tryon. 1960. *Prices and Costs in Manufacturing Industries* (U.S. Cong., Joint Economic Committee, Study Paper No. 17, Materials Prepared in Connection with the Study of Employment, Growth, and Price Levels, 86th Cong., 2d Sess.)

Severo, Richard. 1993. "A.H. Raskin, 82, Times Reporter and Editor, Dies." *N.Y. Times*, Dec. 23, p. A11, col. 1 (nat. ed.)

Sheahan, John. 1967. *The Wage-Price Guideposts.* Washington, D.C.: Brookings

Shelton, William, & John Chandler. 1963a. "International Comparisons of Unit Labor Cost: Concepts and Methods." *Monthly Labor Review* 86 (5):538–47

———. 1963b. "The Role of Cost in Foreign Trade." *Monthly Labor Review* 86 (5):485–90

Sherman, Howard. 1990. *The Business Cycle: Growth and Crisis Under Capitalism.* Princeton: Princeton University

Shonfield, Andrew. 1969 [1965]. *Modern Capitalism: The Changing Balance of Public and Private Power.* London: Oxford University

Skiba, Rainer, & Hermann. Adam. 1974. *Das westdeutsche Lohnniveau zwischen den beiden Weltkriegen und nach der Währungsreform.* Cologne: Bund

Sloan, Alfred. 1965 [1963]. *My Years with General Motors.* New York: MacFadden

Smith, Adam. 1937 [1776]. *An Inquiry into the Nature and Causes of the Wealth of Nations* (Edwin Cannan ed.). New York: Modern Library

Smith, David. 1968. "Incomes Policy." In *Britain's Economic Prospects* 104–44 (Richard Caves et al. eds.). Washington, D.C.: Brookings

Smith, James. 1991. *Brookings at Seventy Five.* Washington, D.C.: Brookings

Solow, Robert. 1960. "Income Inequality Since the War." In *Postwar Economic Trends in the United States* 91–138 (Ralph Freeman ed.). New York: Harper

———. 1966. "The Case Against the Case Against the Guideposts." In *Guidelines, Informal Controls, and the Market Place: Policy Choices in a Full Employment Economy* 41–54 (George Schultz & Robert Aliber eds.). Chicago: University of Chicago

Soule, George. 1922. "The Relation Between Wages and National Productivity." *Annals of the American Academy of Political and Social Science* Vol. C, No. 189:85–90

———. 1923. "The Productivity Factor in Wage Determinations." *American Economic Review* 13 (1):128–40 (Supplement)

———. 1968 [1947]. *Prosperity Decade: From War to Depression: 1917–1929.* New York: Harper

"Spurgeon Bell, An Economist, 88." 1969. *N.Y. Times.* Dec. 20, p. 20, col. 7

Stewart, Ethelbert. 1930. "Ratio of Value of Production to Wages and Their Purchasing Power in Manufacturing Establishments, 1849 to 1929." *Monthly Labor Review* 31 (6):1329–32

Stockett, J. Noble. 1918. *The Arbitral Determination of Railway Wages.* Boston: Houghton Mifflin

Tarnow, Fritz. 1927. "Eine Lohntheorie der amerikanischen Gewerkschaften." *Gewerkschafts-Zeitung*, Sept. 3, pp. 1–3

Taylor, Frederick. 1911. *The Principles of Scientific Management.* New York: Harper
———. 1912. *Shop Management.* New York: Harper
———. 1947 [1912]. *Taylor's Testimony Before the Special House Committee.* In *idem, Scientific Management.* New York: Harper
Thorne, Florence. 1957. *Samuel Gompers—American Statesman.* New York: Philosophical Library
Trussel, C. 1948. "Key Spy Ring Witness Balks." *N.Y. Times,* Oct. 10, p. 1, col. 6
———. 1953. "2 Refuse to Tell If They Are Spies." *N.Y. Times,* May 2, p. 4, col. 3
Uchitelle, Louis. 1987. "How to Gauge Inflation Rate." *N.Y. Times,* July 8, sect. D, p. 2, col. 1
Uhlmann, Luitpold, & Gerhard Huber. 1971. *Technischer und struktureller Wandel in der wachsenden Wirtschaft.* Frankfurt am Main: Europäische Verlagsanstalt
U.S. Bureau of Economic Analysis. 1977. *Handbook of Cyclical Indicators: A Supplement to Business Conditions Digest*
———. 1984. *Handbook of Cyclical Indicators: A Supplement to Business Conditions Digest*
U.S. Bureau of Labor Statistics. 1966. *Bulletin 1518: Unit Labor Cost in Manufacturing: Trends in Nine Countries, 1950–65*
———. 1974. *Bulletin 1825: Handbook of Labor Statistics 1974*
———. 1975. *Bulletin 1865: Handbook of Labor Statistics 1975—Reference Edition*
———. 1983. *Bulletin 2175: Handbook of Labor Statistics*
———. 1986. *Bulletin 2298: Productivity and the Economy: A Chartbook* (Revised)
———. 1992. *Bulletin 2414: BLS Handbook of Methods*
U.S. Bureau of the Census. 1975. *Historical Statistics of the United States, Colonial Times to 1970* (Bicentennial ed.)
U.S. Civil Service Commission. 1942. *Official Register of the United States 1942*
———. 1943. *Official Register of the United States 1943*
———. 1944. *Official Register of the United States 1944*
———. 1945. *Official Register of the United States 1945*
———. 1946. *Official Register of the United States 1946*
U.S. Commissioner of Labor. 1899. *Thirteenth Annual Report. 1898: Hand and Machine Labor*
U.S. Congress. 1951. *Congressional Record* 97 (82nd Cong., 1st Sess.)
———. 1953. *Congressional Record* 99 (83rd Cong., 1st Sess.)
———. 1954. *Congressional Record* 100 (83rd Cong., 2nd Sess.)
———. 1955. *Congressional Record* 101 (84th Cong., 1st Sess.)
———. 1957. *Congressional Record* 103 (85th Cong., 1st Sess.)
———. 1958. *Congressional Record* 104 (85th Cong., 2nd Sess.)
———. 1960. *Congressional Record* 106 (86th Cong., 2nd Sess.)
U.S. Council of Economic Advisers. 1949, 1962, 1964, 1967, 1968, 1974, 1975, 1979, 1980, 1981, 1988, 1992, 1994. *Economic Report of the President*
U.S. House of Representatives. 1939. Report No. 1332: *Studies of Productivity and Labor Costs in Industry.* 76th Cong., 1st Sess.
———. 1922. Committee on Labor. *Hearings on Creating a Board of Adjustment and Board of Appeals for Employees of Navy Yards and Arsenals.* 67th Cong., 2nd Sess.
———. 1948. Committee on Un-American Activities. *Hearings Regarding Espionage in the United States Government.* 80th Cong., 2nd Sess.
———. 1955. *Investigation of Communist Infiltration of Government—Part 1: Hearings.* 84th Cong., 1st Sess.
———. 1956. *Investigation of Communist Infiltration of Government—Part 3: Hearings.* 84th Cong., 2nd Sess.
U.S. Senate. 1952. Subcommittee to Investigate the Administration of the Internal Security Act and Other Internal Security Laws of the Committee on the Judiciary. *Hearings on Institute of Pacific Relations.* 82nd Cong., 2nd Sess.
———. 1953a. *Hearings on Interlocking Subversion in Government Departments.* 83rd Cong., 1st Cong. Pt. 1
———. 1953b. *Interlocking Subversion in Government Departments: Report.* 83rd Cong., 1st Sess. (Committee Print)
———. 1955. Committee on Labor and Public Welfare. *Nomination of Ewan Clague, of Pennsylvania, to Be Commissioner, Bureau of Labor Statistics, U.S. Department of Labor: Hearing.* 84th Cong., 1st Sess.
Vygodskii, S. 1969. *Sovremennyi kapitalizm (opyt teoreticheskogo analiza).* Moscow: Mysl'
"Wage Theories and Arguments: No. 4—Productivity." 1924. *Facts for Workers* 2 (4): 1–2
"Wage Theory and Practice." 1926. *N.Y. Times,* Mar. 1, p. 18, col. 3
Waggaman, Mary. 1923. "Expansion of the 'Family-Wage' System in France and Belgium." *Monthly Labor Review* 17 (4):777–93
———. 1924. "'Family-Wage' System in Germany and Certain Other European Countries." *Monthly Labor Review* 18 (1):20–29
Wagner, Wolf. 1976. *Verelendungstheorie—die hilflose Kapitalismuskritik.* Frankfurt am Main: Fischer

Weber, Arnold.1973. *In Pursuit of Price Stability: The Wage-Price Freeze of 1971*. Washington, D.C.: Brookings

Weintraub, David. 1932. "The Displacement of Workers Through Increases in Efficiency and Their Absorption by Industry, 1920–1931." *Journal of the American Statistical Association* 27 (180):383–400

————, & Harry Magdoff. 1940. "The Service Industries in Relation to Employment Trends." *Econometrica* 8 (4):289–311

Weisskopf, Thomas. 1979. "Marxian Crisis Theory and the Rate of Profit in the Postwar U.S. Economy." *Cambridge Journal of Economics* 3:341–78

White, Michael. 1988. "Prices, Unit Labor Costs, Wages, and Causality in the United States, 1947–1982." *Quarterly Review of Economics and Business* 28 (3):78–87

Who's Who in American Jewry. 1980. Los Angeles: Standard Who's Who

Who's Who in the Socialist Countries of Europe. 1989. Vol. 2 (Juliusz Stroynowski ed.). Munich: Saur

Williams, John. 1945. "Free Enterprise and Full Employment." In *Financing American Prosperity: A Symposium of Economists* 337–90 (Paul Homan & Fritz Machlup eds.). New York: Twentieth Century Fund

Williams, Robert. 1987. *Klaus Fuchs, Atom Spy*. Cambridge: Harvard University

Wolman, Leo. 1936. *Ebb and Flow in Trade Unionism*. New York: National Bureau of Economic Research

Ybarra, Michael. 1994. "Janitors' Union Uses Pressure and Theatrics to Expand Its Ranks." *Wall Street Journal*, Mar. 21, p. 1, col. 6

II
Fatal Subtraction:
Statistical MIAs on the Industrial Battlefield

[W]hen the dead bodies of girls are found piled up against locked doors leading to the exits after a factory fire . . . who wants to hear about a great relief fund? What we want is to start a revolution. . . . If we undertake to stop this unnecessary killing and injuring of workers in the course of industry . . . [t]he first thing we need is . . . complete and accurate information about the accidents that are happening. It seems a tame thing to drop so suddenly from talk of revolutions to talk of statistics. But I believe in statistics just as firmly as I believe in revolutions. And what is more, I believe statistics are good stuff to start a revolution with.[1]

A million workers in the United States have been killed in the line of duty alone since the mid-1920s.[2] Yet not until the Occupational Safety and Health Act of 1970 (OSHA) went into effect were employers generally obligated to "furnish to each of [their] employees employment and a place of employment which are free from recognized hazards that are causing or are likely to cause death or serious physical harm to [their] employees."[3] In order to promote this purpose, Congress ordered the Secretary of Labor to "develop and maintain an effective program of collection, compilation, and analysis of occupational safety and health statistics." Since that time it has been the Department of Labor's duty to "compile accurate statistics on work injuries and illnesses which shall include all disabling, serious, or significant injuries and illnesses, whether or not involving loss of time from work, other than minor injuries."[4]

Yet almost a quarter-century passed before the U.S. government even purported to know how many workers had been killed in the previous year by workplace injuries. The far greater number—estimated at 100,000 annually[5]—succumbing to occupational illnesses and diseases neither the new Census of Fatal Occupational Injuries nor any governmental or private organization pretends to know.[6]

Thus, implausible as it may seem, despite the fact that the last state (Mississippi) enacted a workers' compensation statute almost a half-century ago, the United States still lacks comprehensive and accurate data on work-related fatalities. Public consciousness of the dangerousness of employment is not only underdeveloped, but shaped by and filtered through another agenda. For while the trade press concedes that "[t]he [construction] industry remains unnecessarily dangerous as a whole," its

56

concerns appear to be not those whose lives are prematurely terminated, but employers' profits: a tripling of workers' compensation costs during the past decade is said to be "bleeding the industry dry."[7]

Throughout the twentieth century, one refrain of industrial accident literature has been martial: "War is commonly regarded as the most destructive of human events. But . . . occupational injuries cause far more casualties than war."[8] And if "the workshop is more dangerous than the battle field," then the American industrial battlefield is the most dangerous of all.[9] The leading early twentieth-century U.S. authority on workers' compensation for industrial accidents opened one of his books with an extended comparison between war and peace. Estimating, in the absence of national data, 25,000 deaths annually, E.H. Downey calculated that

> work accidents in the aggregate are equivalent to the losses of a perpetual campaign. Of deaths alone the twelve months' total is four times the number killed and mortally wounded in the battle of Gettysburg. . . . The toll of life and limb exacted during the second decade of the twentieth century exceeds the nation's losses in battle from the Declaration of Independence to the present day.[10]

Significantly, since for Downey it was an "ugly fact . . . that work accidents . . . are due to causes inherent in mechanical industry . . . and in the hereditary traits of human nature," he saw "no prospect that the 'carnage of peace' will be terminated, as the carnage of war may be, within the predictable future." Consequently, just as patriots are fond of measuring the price of a nation's freedom in terms of battle deaths, so, too, consumer sovereignty takes its toll: "every machine-made commodity . . . ha[s] a definite cost in human blood."[11] To be sure, use of the term *accident* stands in jarring juxtaposition to the military imagery: most soldiers are killed intentionally, not accidentally. And the seeming inappropriateness or quasi-oxymoronic character of industrial battlefield rhetoric is intensified in English by the double-meaning of *accident* as unexpected and unintended event on the one hand and injury on the other. But then even between belligerents the same ambiguity attaches to *casualty*.[12]

The rhetorical support mobilized on behalf of national safety legislation in the 1960s resurrected the bloody industrial battlefield imagery of the World War I era. Even President Nixon's new Secretary of Labor, George Shultz, soon to become a high executive at Bechtel Corporation, the world's largest construction firm, captured "the grim current scene" for Congress in a phrase that came to form a refrain in the ensuing debates.[13] Accepting the figure of the National Safety Council (NSC), a private corporate accident prevention organization, that industrial accidents killed 14,000 workers annually, Shultz remarked that: "During the last four years more Americans have been killed where they work than in Vietnam."[14]

In social or natural science investigations it is or should be methodologically self-explanatory that before any phenomenon can be counted, it must be conceptualized and defined.[15] To be sure, certain tricky definitional issues do exist that require clarification before industrial injury fatalities can be counted, but they have largely been resolved or at least disposed of.[16] For many decades, however, the more urgent issue has been for the state to implement adequate injury surveillance in order to conduct an accurate count; the resulting data could then be used for epidemiological studies on the basis of which the state could intervene in employers' operations to impose safer working conditions.[17]

This study analyzes the history of the failure to perform such an enumeration and its consequences for the health and safety of workers in the United States. In order to provide a more finely textured sense of the issues, throughout illustrative material is taken from construction, one of the most dangerous industries.[18] It remains an industry in which researchers seriously explore correlations between the lunar cycle and injuries,[19] and employers are not embarrassed to say that "they're 'expected,' based on insurance premiums, to kill three workers on a large project or that it's 'acceptable' to have one death for every three-fourths of a mile of new tunnel completed."[20]

The study begins with an account of the statistical chaos and confusion engendered by the murderous pace of production at the beginning of the twentieth century. Following a survey of flawed private and government efforts to count the dead at work since the 1920s, the focus shifts to the statistical and enforcement defects of OSHA. After analyzing the fatality trends uncovered by the new Census and a renewed tendency to divert attention from the antagonism between safety and profits, the article concludes with a critique of one important use to which occupational fatality data have been put—economic and legal theories that assert that workers in especially dangerous occupations are compensated for the risks to which they are exposed.

In the Beginning was *Tohu Vabohu*

In the nineteenth century, what was counted was what counted.[21]

By the first decade of the twentieth century, observers had identified a close relationship between the seemingly limitless expansionism of capitalism in the United States and its merciless subordination of all activities to the criterion of profitability. The monomaniacal drive to reduce production costs on which U.S. capital's successful "struggle . . . for international industrial supremacy" and conquest of the world market hinged was in large part made possible by a "stupendous loss" of life.[22] In 1905, Werner Sombart, the German economic historian, according to whose most enduring bon mot all socialist utopias in the United States foundered on "roast beef and apple pie,"[23] was nevertheless impressed by the tendency of unbridled capital accumulation there to assert itself "over dead bodies."[24] The 75,000 railway employees killed during the quarter-century preceding World War I was only the most vivid illustration of the greater speed and lower level of accident prevention characteristic of U.S. enterprise. At the peak of this industrial slaughter, in 1907, 7,776 workers were killed on railroads and in coal mines alone.[25]

U.S. industry during those years "had the reputation of being the most reckless in the world,"[26] and the U.S. Department of Labor found "a frightful disregard of human life. Accident occurrence had reached a condition not paralleled perhaps at any other time or place."[27] Fatality rates in U.S. coal mines were were almost triple those in the United Kingdom and almost double those in Prussia; accident rates among U.S. railway employees were two and one-half times as high as on the German railways.[28] U.S. capital's simultaneous rise to world leadership in industrial production and industrial killing thus instantiated Marx's claim that "capitalist production is . . . most economical of . . . labour realized in commodities. It is a greater spendthrift than any other mode of production of man, of living labour. . . ."[29]

In urging the adoption of injury liability and insurance legislation, Progressives and muckrakers[30] graphically portrayed the human cost of U.S. capitalism's "precious industrial supremacy." Arthur Reeve performed the transatlantic arithmetic: every year "the industrial Juggernaut" drew a million immigrants from Europe to maintain its unprecedented speed, and every year the "sheer brutal carelessness . . . of greedy employers," for whom "[l]aw departments and human life" were cheaper than the cost of accident protection, killed or injured half a million.[31] Crystal Eastman's contribution to *The Pittsburgh Survey* was a landmark account of the fatalities in heavy industry.[32] Upton Sinclair's depiction of the horrifying ways in which industrialized slaughterhouses killed workers as well as animals helped galvanize public opinion—if only to institute federal meat inspection.[33] In his powerful indictment, "Making Steel and Killing Men," William Hard asked: "Must we continue to be obliged to think of scorched and scalded human beings whenever we sit on the back platform of an observation-car and watch the steel rails rolling out behind us?"[34]

Early twentieth-century labor union leaders, echoing *Scientific American,* underscored how much higher per capita industrial fatality rates were

in the United States than in Europe.[35] Samuel Gompers, the president of
the American Federation of Labor, upbraiding "Moloch" for the thousands of annual sacrifices that its "industrial slaughter" claimed,[36] charged
that this toll of "maimed, crippled and killed gives our employing classes
the reputation of being heartless, and even bloody."[37] And the Federation's vice-president, John Mitchell, while conceding that the number of
fatalities and injuries was "not even officially counted" in the United
States, nevertheless drew from the estimates of industrial casualty rates
triple those in Europe the "inevitable conclusion that if it cost more to
kill a workman in America than to protect him, as it does in Europe, the
American workman would not be killed, he would be protected."[38]

A long line of observers has remarked on the extraordinary dangerousness of construction work in the United States, which has accounted
for 15 percent of all occupational fatalities (150,000 since 1933)—about
three times the industry's share of total employment.[39] The International
Association of Bridge and Structural Ironworkers, for example, reported
that one per cent of its membership—109 workers—were killed in accidents in fiscal year 1911–12.[40] (Sixty years later the union was still losing
100 members a year to work-related fatalities.)[41] At the same time, the
premier construction-engineering journal editorially conceded that: "It
must be frankly accepted that the most efficient method of prosecuting
work is not always the safest."[42] Conversely, the "safe builder is . . . put
at a disadvantage in bidding."[43]

In part because the peculiar constellations of class conflict in the
industrializing societies of Western Europe had led already in the nineteenth century to the imposition of certain statutory—albeit often weakly
enforced—duties on employers to protect their employees from workplace
dangers,[44] representatives of organized labor from other countries were
also impressed by the dearth of safety precautions in the United States.
During his visit to the United States shortly before World War I, the
chairman of the General Commission of the German Free Trade Unions
noted the lack of protective measures on skyscrapers, which led the industry to reckon with one death per story. Compared with German workers,
who in Carl Legien's opinion had already eliminated the worst abuses,
U.S. workers had the capacity to achieve much more through legislation.
But "human life on the other side of the big pond is apparently given
little value, social feeling has not yet become the common good of the
progressive working class."[45]

Coming from the representative of a national working class that had
recorded more than 115,000 industrial fatalities during the first 18 years
of operation of Bismarck's accident insurance law, this judgment was not
made lightly.[46] But Legien's observations also reflected the fact that the
working class in the United States before World War I, still "dumb-

founded by the noise of production," as it were, had not yet "come to" and initiated resistance[47] to the deterioration of working conditions brought on by the task compression, deskilling, and speed-ups associated with the new industrial drive system.[48] The combined impact of labor-saving mechanization and the massive growth of an increasingly ethnically divided labor supply resulting from the unprecedented volume of immigration created such a large "standing army of the unemployed" even during periods of prosperity[49] that even labor unions did "not feel strong enough to enforce demands which would involve large outlays by employers for safe equipment and other improvements."[50]

Thus of the strikes at more than 40,000 building trades establishments during the last two decades of the nineteenth century, only one was "for better arrangements for safety"; the comparable total among 15,000 coal and coke establishments was only seven.[51] Workers and their unions had to wait more than a half-century for the kind of federal statute that could impose national safety standards on firms and thus preclude the competitive race to the bottom with which employers are wont to threaten employees as the result of union demands for better working conditions.[52] Speculating that he could shift the costs of reproducing the working class to the workers themselves, other firms, or the next generation of capitalists, the individual Marxist capitalist "rebell[ed] constantly against the aggregate interest of the capitalist class."[53] In the meantime, even for the United Mine Workers safety issues remained peripheral to maintaining the union's strength.[54]

These international comparative impressionistic accounts appear to accord with the available data. In the United Kingdom, for example, which has maintained a much more centralized yet far from all-inclusive or uniform statistical collection system since the mid-nineteenth-century,[55] during the entire period from 1896 to 1991, total recorded construction fatalities amounted to only about 16,000.[56] The construction industry in the United States, with a population two to four times as large during the twentieth century, may have produced fifteen to twenty times as many deaths. At the end of the twentieth century, U.S. industrial fatality rates in general and in construction in particular remain international outliers.[57]

In fact, however, no one in the early twentieth century knew how many industrial soldiers were being mortally wounded each year in the United States. If the state apparatus counts only what counts, then apparently "[n]o one seem[ed] to care very much if we do kill more people in one year of peace than were slain and wounded throughout the terrible Russo-Japanese war."[58] A striking manifestation of this apparent insouciance and the chief technical reason for this nescience was the lack of any statutory obligation for employers to report workplace fatalities in any state until the 1880s; and even thereafter such duties were limited and poorly enforced.[59] The individual state factory inspectors' reports were not only "very defective," but also so lacking in uniformity as to "preclude[] the possibility of accurate interstate comparison."[60] Despite congressional enactments requiring railroads to report injuries to the Interstate Commerce Commission and subjecting them to money penalties for noncompliance,[61] not even this oldest and most complete series was entirely trustworthy.[62]

Reeve's proposal in 1907 that the states require all accidents to be reported to their labor bureaus and that the federal Department of Commerce and Labor process national tabulations[63] was one whose time has still not come at the end of the century. Bereft of a mandatory-institutionalized infrastructure, even government agencies were reduced to speculation. Thus the U.S. Bureau of Labor published a guesstimate based on fragmentary data of 17,500 in 1908[64] followed by another of 25,000 in 1915;[65] at the same time the U.S. Commission on Industrial Relations reported a figure of 35,000.[66] Yet the following year the U.S. Commissioner of Labor Statistics readily conceded that "[i]ndustrial accident statistics for the United States do not exist,"[67] and a decade later his successor repeated the profession and laments of ignorance.[68]

The wave of enactments of workers' compensation legislation in about three-fourths of the states between 1911 and U.S. entry into World War I[69] should, in theory, have created a source of broad (though by no means comprehensive) and accurate data on work-related fatalities on the basis of which prevention programs could have been developed. Unlike the Bismarckian insurance scheme, which preceded U.S. laws by three decades,[70] the various state workers' compensation statutes, however, failed to generate a nationally uniform reporting system.[71] Thus estimates of 10,000 to 12,000 annual fatalities for 1917 to 1919 based on aggregating state workers' compensation claims were accompanied by disclaimers of inadequacy, incompleteness, and noncomparability.[72]

Despite the lack of comprehensive statistics, management was well aware that construction work, with fatality and serious injury rates running in excess of four times those in factories, was "extra hazardous." Editorializing under the ambiguous title, "Unwarranted Accident Waste in Construction," *Engineering News-Record*, the industry's principal trade journal, observed toward the close of World War I that: "Casualties on the battle front in France exhibit hardly a worse record of fatalities."[73] The owner of the leading skyscraper construction firm confirmed at the end of the boom of the 1920s that over the previous ten-year period, one steel erector died for every thirty-three hours of employed time.[74]

In the early 1920s, the U.S. Bureau of Labor Statistics (BLS), using a highly speculative set of assumptions, estimated annual industrial fatalities at 30,039.[75] This pseudo-precision did not mislead the Secretary of Labor, who noted in his annual report that: "It is not greatly to the credit of our people that nobody knows . . . even the annual number of industrial fatalities."[76] The lack of federal regulation or oversight of working conditions before the New Deal was in large part responsible for the lack of any nationally uniform labor statistics.[77] In order to make a small start toward abating this ignorance—an initiative that did not even rise to the level of government information-gathering as an aid to legislation[78]—bills were filed in both houses of Congress in 1926 to establish a division of safety within the BLS to collect and analyze data on industrial accidents "with special reference to their causes, effects, and occupational distribution."[79] The chief sponsor in the House of Representatives, continuing the tradition of military metaphors, suggested "that many great battles of the world have not caused so many casualties as perhaps one year of industry in the United States."[80] That the bill was never enacted and the division of safety therefore not created can in part be accounted for by the dizzy-with-success free enterprise of the 1920s, legislatively embodied by Senator Hiram Bingham. A former history professor at Yale and governor of Connecticut, he contended that workers' compensation statutes had literally eliminated all problems:

> "[I]n Connecticut . . . [w]e passed an employer's liability compensation act, which requires all employers . . . to see to it that their employees should be protected at work. Now, this had the very natural effect of making the manufacturers do what they should have done before, look into the causes of their own accidents and guard against them. [T]his is the proper theory of government, to put on the individual the initiative of seeing to it that he corrects his own errors, rather than to have the Government tell him what he must do in order to correct them, and that is the reason, I take it, why we do not find it necessary to collect accident statistics any more; it is because the workmen are protected, and the manufacturers themselves are seeing to it that they can and do establish the very latest form of safety devices, for their own protection, and for the saving in insurance, and for the safety of their workers.
>
> "The thing works out there in the proper way.[81]

Such market-knows-best anti-paternalism[82] carried the day during the "New Capitalism" of the Republican ascendancy, prefiguring the emergence of an econometrically sophisticated market-inspired critique of state intervention a half-century later.[83] Senator Bingham's opposition ultimately caused the bill to fail, but even business knew better than to trust such mechanistic wishful thinking.[84] Thus at the height of the boom, just days before the stock market crash, William Wheeler, one of construction management's safety spokesmen, observed that "[t]his human

sacrifice, chargeable to the industry, is unnecessary and avoidable." However, "[h]umanitarianism is not required to tell contractors what to do
when an economic need, rather an economic justification for it, is clearly
shown." That economic basis was simply that "the industry pays alto-
gether too large an accident bill which represents pure waste of productive
capital." Yet in trying to identify the financial incentives that would moti-
vate construction firms to pursue safety measures, Wheeler specified for
the Annual Safety Congress of the National Safety Council (NSC) how
"all accidents are 'caused'":

> Progressive and successful contractors . . . have learned that the most im-
> portant thing in the building industry is TIME; that material and men must
> be kept moving *without loss of time* if a building is to be ready on the contem-
> plated date; and also, that *all* of their equipment, labor and capital must be
> used *all of the time* if maximum profits are to be counted. The tenor of the
> present day building business is unrelenting competition, fast production
> with rising pressure upon personnel and equipment. This is a fast moving
> era and speed is its urge. The business of today that succeeds must move
> fast. . . .[85]

Wheeler was merely localizing in construction the larger truth about
the "Penalty the American Nation Pays for Speed."[86] The BLS agreed
that the fact that "[b]oth contractor and owner are apt to be anxious to
push the job with all practicable speed" was among the factors "conspir[-
ing] to render difficult the task of securing a reasonable degree of
safety."[87] Unsurprisingly, then, in the depths of the Great Depression,
the National Conference on Construction, through its Committee on
Elimination of Waste and Undesirable Practices, conceded that "the industry has no practical plan for accident prevention" despite the fact that
knowledge of "the real causes of the accidents" was available.[88]
Despite the carnage that capital in construction and elsewhere was
leaving in its wake, data remained sparse. Echoing complaints that it had
already voiced during the heady 1920s,[89] the BLS acknowledged at the
beginning of the New Deal that:

> Accurate information on industrial injuries in the United States is unfor-
> tunately not available. Not only is it impossible to determine with any degree
> of accuracy the causes of accidents, the nature of the injuries, the extent of
> the disabilities, the number of workers handicapped through injury, or the
> cost in time or money lost through industrial injuries, but even the most
> elementary part of information relating to industrial injuries—the total num-
> ber of disabling injuries sustained by industrial workers within a given year—
> is not available for the country as a whole.
> It would seem to be a rather simple matter to determine the number of
> fatal and nonfatal injuries in each State and combine these in a complete

tabulation. This, however, has not been possible, partly through lack of reporting in States which have not adopted workmen's compensation laws or from industries not covered by the law in other States.[90]

By the end of the 1930s, when construction was "by far the most hazardous" industry,[91] the BLS may still not have had precise figures, but it knew enough to add a new twist to the rhetoric of *bellum accidentum:* "The number of workers killed at their jobs during 1937 was more than 4 times the number of soldiers killed during the entire Revolutionary War."[92]

The National Safety Council: "Safety First"—and Accuracy Last[93]

There is no step, no forward step made by what we call the proletariat, the working population, against the power-holding class except in one way. . . . [O]rganized labor, the organized proletariat, the organized—whatever you may please to call it—has never won a substantial victory over that power-holding class, except in one way, and that is upon the Christian or moral right, and that can lick the hard boiled and the standpatters.[94]

In the absence of any general-purpose national industrial safety and health legislation, the federal government lacked an institutionalized inspection, enforcement, or insurance compensation basis for generating statistics. In this statutory vacuum it was only appropriate that laissez faire guided data collection as well as the labor market. As a symbolic remnant of the divergent national paths to industrial injury prevention, the *Statistical Abstract of the United States* continues to report the number of "workers killed" in the section headed, "Labor Force, Employment, and Earnings,"[95] whereas the corresponding statistical compendia in Europe place these data under such rubrics as "Public Health," "Insurance," or "Social Conditions."[96]

Consistent with the voluntary character of the U.S. approach, from the 1930s until the enactment of OSHA, the generation of data on employment-related fatalities largely rested with a private organization, the NSC, which compiled such statistics as part of its overall "Safety First" accident prevention program. The NSC was chartered by an act of Congress in 1953,[97] four decades after it emerged from efforts by the murderous steel industry to manage its casualties and by big business in general to ward off even more costly and less predictable injury indemnification systems than workers' compensation laws.[98] For many years, the NSC has been the key organization in a private network designed to enable employers to preempt state intervention by voluntarily formulating and adopting their own safety and health standards. As "a captive of its member firms . . . it function[s] as a public relations agency and corporate think tank rather than an independent research body. [T]he NSC develop[s] and promote[s] preventive strategies that coincide[] with corporate control of production, personnel relations, and plant operations."[99]

The NSC based (and continues to base) its estimates of industrial fatality on death certificates compiled by the National Center for Health Statistics and annual reports by state registrars of vital statistics. Although death certificates "in theory" contain the information required to categorize all fatalities into the four classes (motor vehicle, work, home, and public) which form the NSC's universe of accidental death, "[i]n practice . . . missing or incompletely coded information prevents the direct use of death certificate data for determining the class totals" other than motor vehicles.[100] Moreover, the death certificates do not specify the industries in which the deaths occurred. In order to rectify this defect:

> From the late 1930's to the mid-60's a statistician from the Council would go to Washington in January or February of each year to meet with statisticians at . . . BLS . . . and other federal agencies collecting accident-related data. Together they would go over the latest information from BLS surveys, Council estimates, reports from Council members, and special studies, and they would agree on the work death total that both agencies would use. They would also agree on the distribution of those deaths among the major industry groups.[101]

The only light that the NSC chooses to shine into this densely black methodological box is a table showing what was apparently the last "reconciliation" between the NSC and the BLS in 1964. For the construction industry, where non-employees accounted for between a quarter and a fifth of all fatalities, the data were based on "small sample surveys" conducted by the BLS.[102] If this procedure was murky and suspected of including duplicate deaths, which rendered both absolute levels and year-to-year changes unreliable,[103] since the mid-1960s, when the BLS ceased furnishing the NSC with the annual benchmarks derived from BLS surveys, it has become impenetrable. This incomprehensibility is only enhanced by the procedure that the NSC devised to "allocate" deaths to the three non-motor vehicle classes. Called "the 3-Way Split," it applies a "set of allocation factors" to each combination of age-group and external cause of death derived from a survey of death certificates; developed in the 1930s, these factors were based on documentation which is no longer available to the NSC, although it asserts that a recent revision did not call for a re-estimation of total workplace deaths.[104]

The following colloquy between the president of the NSC and Harrison Williams, the chairman of the Senate Committee on Labor and Public Welfare, inadvertently highlighted the NSC's opaque methodology:

> The CHAIRMAN. You have some statistics here that we have been unable to get on the . . . numbers of deaths due to accident. Where do you get your statistics? The Labor Department doesn't have them?
> Mr. TOFANY. We get them from a variety of sources including the agencies of the Federal Government and private sector organizations, the data that flows from them and correlate them. For example, the total number of deaths that happened into [sic] the country are broken down into categories as to cause of death. And to the extent they can apply that information, that works its way into the conclusions our statisticians reach.
> Thus, we have a wide variety of sources which we utilize to the extent that we can in order to develop the relationship of all of the data as it relies to a given accident area where we don't have the specific report, per se, and then——[105]

One reason that Williams, arguably the staunchest congressional advocate of labor-protective legislation during the post-World War II period, failed to challenge or even to remark on this double talk may have been that the NSC's high industrial fatality figures provided ongoing justification for strengthening OSHA.[106] Although the BLS, in compliance with the Secretary of Labor's statutory duty to develop injury statistics under OSHA, began to operate under a scope of coverage and definitions which were incompatible with the NSC's, and despite the lack of any "other direct measures of fatality experience," the NSC has "continued to carry forward these estimates." For public consumption, the NSC contends "that this procedure is the most satisfactory now available."[107] Privately, however, the manager of the NSC's statistics department concedes that the NSC's annual estimates, cut off from periodic benchmarking, began to "deviate from reality" by the end of the 1970s. Moreover, the NSC continues to publish data on absolute levels of fatalities without caveats although the data for at least the last three decades reflect only year-to-year changes.[108]

This bewildering methodology is all the more bizarre given the NSC's eminently practical purposes as "the leader of the voluntary safety movement, integrating the views of management, labor, government, and the general public." After all, in order to spotlight growing problems and to deemphasize sources of accidents of decreasing importance, the NSC depends on "complete, consistent, comparable, unbiased, and current" data, which it contends are available through selection of sources and procedures that "maximize" such reliability.[109] The NSC's continued dissemination of data based on statistical adjustments that became obsolete almost three decades ago calls into question its claim that "[c]redibility" is one of its "hallmarks."[110] Similarly, the NSC's nonfatal injury statistics, collected voluntarily from member firms, are biased because those self-reporting firms compete for safety awards based on their own data.[111]

Despite their manifest defects, the NSC data remain the only long-term comprehensive series, and retain their political value as having furnished the most impressive statistical support that proponents of OSHA could muster. The NSC figures were, for example, the source of the congressional testimony by the president of the AFL-CIO Building and Construction Trades Department that more than 25,000 building tradesmen had been killed on the job during the 1960s.[112] Congress was also animated by the NSC's overall estimates of 2.2 million disabling injuries annually—which may have represented only one-fifth of the actual number[113]—and more than 14,000 fatalities,[114] which may have been an overestimate. The role played by the NSC's data is ironic[115] in light of Ralph Nader's allegations at the 1969 OSHA hearings that the NSC's injury frequency data are "widely recognized as incomplete, often inaccurate, and always unverified" and that "[t]he record of the National Safety Council is impressive in terms of misrepresenting the true safety record of its own members."[116]

The NSC series reveals an astounding total of 862,900 killed during the six decades from 1932 to 1992, 147,400 of whom worked in construction (table 1, p. 69). Moreover, for the forty-five years following World War II, construction fatalities showed a stubbornly irreducible floor: from 1946 to 1990, annual fatalities moved within a very narrow range, never falling below 2,100 or rising above 2,800. This constancy may, however, at least since OSHA's enactment, have been a mere statistical artifact—a function of the fact that NSC has continued to moor its fatality data to an obsolete BLS benchmark. Among the 265,000 workers killed even under the aegis of OSHA, the 50,000 deaths in the construction industry figured prominently.

Joint Private-Public Underestimates

Death entails a total cessation of labor power. . . .[117]

The BLS, too, published survey-based fatality data from 1936 on although the samples outside of manufacturing, mining, and railroads were so fragmentary that the BLS itself did not regard them as "satisfactorily representative." In construction, for example, the BLS went through the motions of extrapolating totals from a mere 148 establishments "because so little information is available . . . from any other source and . . . injury hazards . . . are known to be great."[118] The BLS gradually

Table 1
Workers Killed in the United States, 1928-1992 (NSC)

Year	Total	Construction	Year	Total	Construction
1928	19000	2600	1961	13500	2300
1929	20000	NA	1962	13700	2400
1930	19000	NA	1963	14200	2500
1931	17500	NA	1964	14200	2600
1932	15000	1800	1965	14100	2700
1933	14500	2300	1966	14500	2800
1934	16000	2300	1967	14200	2700
1935	16500	2500	1968	14300	2800
1936	18500	2800	1969	14300	2800
1937	19000	3100	1970	13800	2800
1938	16000	2700	1971	13700	2700
1939	15500	1800	1972	14000	2800
1940	17000	3100	1973	14300	2800
1941	18000	3300	1974	13500	2600
1942	18000	3100	1975	13000	2300
1943	17500	2400	1976	12500	2100
1944	16000	1800	1977	12900	2400
1945	16500	1700	1978	13100	2600
1946	16500	2200	1979	13000	2600
1947	17000	2400	1980	13200	2500
1948	16000	2500	1981	12500	2300
1949	15000	2100	1982	11900	2100
1950	15500	2300	1983	11700	2100
1951	16000	2500	1984	11500	2200
1952	15000	2400	1985	11500	2200
1953	15000	2500	1986	11100	2100
1954	14000	2400	1987	11300	2200
1955	14200	2500	1988	11000	2200
1956	14300	2600	1989	10900	2100
1957	14200	2500	1990	10100	2100
1958	13300	2400	1991	9300	1800
1959	13800	2500	1992	8500	1300
1960	13800	2400			

Sources: Construction 1928: R. Fortney & Alvan Battey, *Where the Fatalities Occurred in 1929*, NAT'L SAFETY NEWS, Feb. 1931, at 23, 24; Total 1928-1992: NSC, ACCIDENT FACTS 1993 EDITION 26-27 (1993); Construction 1933-1992: NSC, ACCIDENT FACTS (annually, 1933-1993)

enlarged the samples, and as of 1937 began including self-employeds.[119] Exactly how it collected these sample data the BLS failed to reveal. It appears that until 1938, the BLS obtained the data from state workers' compensation boards, whereas from 1939 on it effected "a drastic change" by switching to voluntary direct reporting by employers.[120] Which source generated more underreporting the BLS did not note or perhaps even examine. By the early post-World War II period, fewer than a third of the construction firms from which the BLS requested data filed usable reports.[121] Such self-selection may well have resulted in undersampling of employers with the worst safety records and thus in underestimates of total fatalities.

These sampling problems notwithstanding, the BLS data appear in fact to have derived at least in part from the NSC tabulations although the BLS did not always make this connection clear. On the one hand, the BLS stated that its work-injury data were based on survey samples of voluntarily participating employers "computed by direct expansion to represent the probable volume of injuries in the total working population."[122] On the other hand, these data "also served the important internal function of supporting the estimates" of annual fatalities,[123] which, especially in the post-World War II years, were the same as the NSC's figures.[124] In 1951, the BLS revealed that since these estimates were "prepared cooperatively" by the two organizations, they were "identical."[125] As the U.S. Commissioner of Labor Statistics explained to the President's Conference on Occupational Safety in 1954 in a "quasi-dramatic presentation," because the BLS "cannot obtain anywhere a complete count of work injuries . . . the technical people" at the BLS and NSC "assemble all of these bits and pieces of work-injury data, fit them together like pieces in a jigsaw puzzle, . . . match them up . . . , and make adjustments so that the figures will be comparable."[126]

In 1966, shortly before the BLS broke off its cooperation with the NSC, it published its first *Handbook of Methods*, which managed to be almost as cryptic about their joint estimation procedures as the NSC. The annual data

> represent the combined judgment of the technical staffs of the two organizations based on a pooling of all data available to either group.
>
> In the absence of a centralized system of reporting work injuries in the United States, the accumulation of data providing national totals must be based upon the assembly of a many bits of data drawn from a wide variety of sources. These basic data frequently overlap or omit entirely certain segments of employment. Additional problems are introduced by a lack of uniformity in the reporting and compilation procedures of the organizations from which the basic data are obtained.[127]

After obliquely conceding that its methods could not be reproduced, checked, or verified, the BLS identified state workers' compensation agencies as the primary data sources although they failed to "meet current needs" because of variations in coverage and inadequate statistical procedures. The BLS therefore had recourse to organizations as heterogeneous as the Coast Guard and the Portland Cement Association to fill in the gaps. Ultimately, only the data for mining, manufacturing, and railroads were deemed "very comprehensive and . . . having a high degree of accuracy," whereas those for agriculture were "fragmentary . . . and may reflect a comparatively high degree of error."[128]

The preceding historical sketch of BLS-NSC cooperation with regard to the creation of industrial accident fatality data should be viewed in the context of the nationally uniform method that the BLS and employers jointly adopted in the 1930s for recording and reporting work injuries. Like the NSC-BLS methodology for fatal injuries, the American Standard Method of Measuring and Recording Work Injury Experience of the American National Standards Institute (ANSI) failed to create accurate data on nonfatal injuries. The ANSI Z16.1 standard inevitably underestimated injuries by excluding from the definition of the "day of disability" the day of injury and the day on which the injured worker returned to full-time work. This distortion, which vitiated all BLS injury data from the 1930s until the enactment of OSHA in 1970, was compounded by a system of voluntary reporting, which presumably biased the sample toward firms with low rates.[129] These methodological machinations formed the basis of Ralph Nader's charge at the OSHA hearings in 1969 that in the 1930s the BLS began intentionally to understate nonfatal accidents by acquiescing in industry's request that certain injuries be excluded and the sample be kept statistically insignificant in order to minimize the visibility of safety problems and industry's responsibility for them.[130] Under the more comprehensive OSHA standard, however, which includes injuries that require medical treatment beyond first aid but do not involve lost workdays, the number of recorded occupational injuries and illnesses more than tripled.[131]

The State Counts Too

The Bureau of Labor Statistics at the request of OSHA doesn't know what the hell is going on. . . . We don't know how many people get killed in construction, much less injured, ill or otherwise.[132]

For the period since the enactment of OSHA, the BLS has issued an alternative series of annual "industrial battle bulletins, which enumer-

Table 2
Workers Killed in the United States, 1971-1991 (BLS-OSHA)

Year	Total	Construction	Year	Total	Construction
1971	4200*	800*	1982	4090	720
1972	5500	1500	1983	3100	670
1973	5700	1000	1984	3740	660
1974	5900	1200	1985	3750	980
1975	5300	1000	1986	3610	670
1976	4500	800	1987	3400	820
1977	4760	NA**	1988	3270	850
1978	4590	925	1989	3600	780
1979	4950	960	1990	2900	700
1980	4400	839	1991	2800	500
1981	4370	800			

Sources: 1971-1973: U.S. BLS, Bull. 1798: OCCUPATIONAL INJURIES AND ILLNESSES BY INDUSTRY: JULY 1 - DECEMBER 31, 1971, tab. 4 at 13 (1973); U.S. BLS, Bull. 1830: OCCUPATIONAL INJURIES AND ILLNESSES BY INDUSTRY, 1972, tab. 5 at 66 (1974); U.S. BLS, Bull. 1830: OCCUPATIONAL INJURIES AND ILLNESSES BY INDUSTRY, 1973, tab. 6 at 73 (1975); 1974-1977: U.S. BLS, Rep. 460: CHARTBOOK ON OCCUPATIONAL INJURIES AND ILLNESSES, 1974, tab. 4 at 25 (1976); U.S. BLS, Rep. 501: CHARTBOOK ON OCCUPATIONAL INJURIES AND ILLNESSES, 1975, tab. 3 at 30 (1977); U.S. BLS, Rep. 535: CHARTBOOK ON OCCUPATIONAL INJURIES AND ILLNESSES, 1976, tab. 4 at 32 (1978) 1978-1991: U.S. BLS, Office of Safety, Health, & Working Conditions (Feb. 7, 1994) (furnished to author).
*Covered only July 1-Dec. 31
**BLS did not publish industry-level fatality data in 1977.[1]

---

[1]BLS offered no express reason for its omission of industry-level fatalities for 1977 or for its resumed publication of such data in 1978. U.S. BLS, Bull. 2078: OCCUPATIONAL INJURIES AND ILLNESSES IN THE UNITED STATES BY INDUSTRY, 1978, at 6-7 (1980).

ate the wounded and killed of the industrial army."[133] These data were, at least until the advent of the Census of Fatal Occupational Injuries for 1992, the quasi-official figures, which were included in the annual report which OSHA requires the President to transmit to Congress.[134] The data that the BLS has collected for the Occupational Safety and Health Administration (OSHAdm) since the second half of 1971 are based on mail surveys of covered employers. Firms, which have no legal duty to respond, report the recordable injuries and illnesses—fatalities, other lost workday cases, and non-lost workday cases resulting in "transfer to another job or termination of employment," or involve "loss of consciousness or restriction of work or motion"[135]—that they are statutorily required to enter into their OSHA logs, although one-quarter fail to comply with that obligation or underrecord and underreport injuries.[136]

The BLS itself has obliquely pointed to the key weakness of its data collection procedure—namely, that the logs "reflect the year's injury and illness experience, *and also* the employer's understanding of the types of cases to record under current recordkeeping guidelines."[137] Yet in order to preserve confidentiality and maintain voluntary participation, the BLS neither validates these reports at the workplace nor shares them with the OSHAdm for inspection and compliance purposes.[138] The BLS's sampling system of unmonitored employer self-reporting prompted occupational medicine and public health scholars to criticize the Bureau's single-source-generated fatality figures as "grossly underreported."[139]

An effective health and safety surveillance program would encompass mass processing and auditing of the logs by the OSHAdm on a scale at least comparable to the Internal Revenue Service's treatment of self-reported income tax forms. But just as Congress has provided for checks on taxpayer truthfulness by requiring employers, banks, and other payors to file corroborating forms, mandating joint maintenance of the logs by unions or other worker representatives would reduce the frequency of self-serving understatements by employers. The effectiveness of the resulting set of accurate statistics would also be significantly enhanced if they were published for each firm so that current and prospective employees would at least have the requisite information for making rational decisions as to where to work, how high their wages should be, and whether changes in working conditions are appropriate.[140]

OSHA, however, is merely a mandatory recordkeeping, not a mandatory reporting system.[141] Indeed, so far removed is OSHA from such a strict regime that an employer, whose only obligation is to make the logs available to the Department of Labor on request,[142] can—without being sanctioned for filing a frivolous claim[143]—judicially challenge the Department's power even to inspect those logs.[144] Moreover, a change in the OSHAdm's enforcement policy gave manufacturing employers a considerable incentive to underreport injuries on their logs. Beginning in 1981, OSHAdm inspectors terminated on-site general schedule (random) inspections as soon as they determined, based on the employer's logs, that the firm's lost work-day injury rate (excluding fatal injuries) was lower than the national average for manufacturing.[145] Such underreporting of lost workdays stems from the widespread practice among employers of "keeping 'the walking wounded' on the job," which less than subtly informs workers that "non-lost-time accidents and first aid accidents are expected" as a matter of course.[146]

The close connection between conceptually deficient accident/injury statistics and prevention is captured by the incompatibility between the construction industry's programmatic approach to safety and OSHA's data reporting system. The Associated General Contractors of America, a large trade organization, made this commonsensical observation in its construction accident prevention manual almost seventy years ago: "An accident is an unintentional interruption to an orderly process—a turning aside of an intended procedure. The injury to persons is only the evidence of an accident."[147] Yet under OSHA, employers are not required to report even major accidents provided that no one is injured.[148] The absurdity of this type of nonreporting was underscored when twenty-eight construction workers died in 1987 as a result of a building collapse in Bridgeport, Connecticut. The same firm that was building L'Ambiance Plaza had previously built Metro Center, thirty miles away, which also collapsed, but because only one worker suffered an injury—the threshold for reporting within 48 hours is a fatality or five injuries[149]—the firm was not required to report it.[150] If OSHAdm had been notified of this previous major construction failure, "we're pretty certain that L'Ambiance never would have occurred."[151]

For the period July 1, 1971 through 1991, the BLS-OSHA series estimated a total of 88,430 fatalities (table 2, p. 72).[152] This figure significantly understated workplace deaths because after 1977 the BLS published fatality data only for establishments with eleven or more employees.[153] The BLS limited the scope of the survey because it reduced the sample by 85,000 "in response to the Presidential directive on reduction of the paperwork burden in survey operations. The sample reduction results in larger sampling errors in the fatality data (statistically rare occurrences), making year-to-year comparisons for this group of small employers of questionable reliability." Based on estimates of annual fatalities among employing units with 10 or fewer employees for the years prior to 1977, the BLS suggested that 800 fatalities be added to the totals for later years.[154] Making this adjustment for the 15 years from 1977 to 1991 would add 12,000 deaths, bringing the total for the 19.5 years of the survey to almost exactly 100,000 fatalities.

Because a recent study shows that the exclusion of small firms may be a greater source of underestimation than previously recognized, the BLS's small-firm adjustment is almost certainly insufficient. A computer analysis of 500,000 safety-inspection records by the *Wall Street Journal* revealed that from 1988 to 1992, 4,337 workers died at workplaces with fewer than twenty employees, whereas only 127 died at those with more than 2,500 employees. The ratio of the fatality rates in the two groups was almost 500 to 1.[155]

For construction alone, the BLS-OSHA surveys showed 17,174 deaths for these two decades or almost one-fifth of all fatalities (table 2). The annual average of about 880 was little more than a third of the 2,300 annual fatalities recorded by the NSC for the same period.[156] This discrepancy has in part been explained by a controlled experiment, which revealed a cluster of non-reporting of fatalities to the OSHAdm among construction firms.[157] In addition, whereas the NSC does not discriminate against dead self-employeds, OSHA covers only employees.[158] Despite all these flaws, an OSHAdm contractee certified the BLS survey as "the only reliable national measure of occupational injury and illness."[159]

A third fatality data base is built on the work-related deaths that employers are required to report to the OSHAdm.[160] These fatalities have run considerably higher than the BLS figures. The 4,792 construction deaths reported to OSHA from 1985 through 1989 exceed the BLS survey results by 17 percent.[161] The discrepancy is to be expected given the BLS survey's many exclusions. By the same token, however, both OSHA and BLS data are underestimates because firms may underreport, and neither agency's reports include the formally self-employed, who are numerous in construction, or workers not covered by OSHA or covered by other safety legislation.[162] By using death certificates and medical examiner records, researchers have discovered that OSHA fatality reports capture only one third of all occupational injury deaths.[163] Death certificates alone, however, also underestimate total occupational fatalities.[164]

Yet a fourth estimate of fatalities is derived from the National Institute for Occupational Safety and Health (NIOSH) National Traumatic Occupational Fatalities (NTOF) surveillance system for the years 1980 to 1989. Based on death certificates from state vital statistics agencies which are estimated as identifying 80 percent of work-related fatalities, NTOF reported 11,417 construction fatalities during the 1980s. The annual average of 1,142 deaths is about 50 percent and 20 percent higher than the BLS and OSHA figures respectively, and about one-half of the NSC total. According to the NTOF study, the fatal injury rate in construction during the 1980s, 25.6 per 100,000 full-time workers, was almost four times the all-industry average.[165] One of the principal reasons for the discrepancy between the NTOF data on the one hand and the BLS/OSHA on the other is the former's inclusion of the nominally self-employed.[166]

A Census of Death Comes to Life

There is no "gold standard" for counting the number of work-related . . . injury deaths.[167]

Thus despite many years of intensive public-private cooperation, estimates of total work-related deaths have varied widely, with the NSC's figures exceeding those of the BLS by a factor of three.[168] As late as the 1980s, medical researchers confirmed that "a complete series of fatal occupational work injuries (all those in a specified time period for a defined population or geographic area) has never been described. In large part, this is because no single source of data permits easy identification of all cases."[169]

The BLS itself "had doubts about the quality" of its own annual estimates of fatalities. One key flaw in the data, as a Government Accounting Office study revealed, was, predictably enough, employers' unpoliced underestimates of injuries as recorded on their OSHA logs.[170] The BLS therefore commissioned a study in the mid-1980s by the National Research Council, which "found it rather startling that an agreed-upon method has not been devised to estimate a phenomenon as basic as traumatic death in the [American] workplace."[171] Since the BLS excluded from its annual survey entities employing fewer than eleven employees and accounting for one-third of total employment, it is unclear why the BLS was startled by this finding—especially since its methodology has otherwise been subject to sharp attack.[172]

Years of critique and self-critique finally resulted in a new approach, which broke both with surveys based on employer self-reporting and with methodologically inscrutable estimates. Twenty-three years after OSHA's enactment, the BLS published the first national Census of Fatal Occupational Injuries with data for 1992. Relying on multiple sources such as death certificates, reports by coroners and medical examiners, and autopsy, workers' compensation, OSHA, state motor vehicle, and news media reports, the Census aspires to be a complete enumeration, the accuracy of which is supposed to be secured by the requirement that a fatality be identified by at least two sources. In keeping with the comprehensive scope of the Census, its aggregate fatality figure of 6,083 includes 1,216 workplace homicides and suicides. Since the NSC's focus on "accidental deaths" excludes such acts, the 4,867 non-intentional fatalities counted by the Census amounted to only 57 percent of the NSC's total of 8,500 for 1992, whereas the 903 enumerated construction fatalities fell 30 percent short of the NSC figure.[173]

This discrepancy suggests either that the Census is less than comprehensive or that the NSC, despite its reputation as a tool of big business, has been exaggerating industrial fatalities. Those responsible for compiling the NSC and Census fatality statistics tentatively agree that the correct figure lies somewhere between the two. They believe, for example, that the Census may be missing work-related transportation fatalities that involve vehicles that are not obviously identifiable to the police or medical authorities as having been driven by workers in the course of their employment. Where, in addition, the dead were nonemployees, who are statutorily excluded from workers' compensation, or were for any other reason outside the scope of such state programs, neither a death certificate nor workers' compensation report would identify such fatalities.[174]

As these enumeration problems demonstrate, the recent intensification of efforts by employers to treat workers as nonemployees in order to lower costs[175] may also be contributing to an underreporting of industrial fatalities. Although it may be unclear how a dead self-employee would comply with a statutory duty to record and notify the OSHAdm of his own death, the exclusion of alleged nonemployees from OSHA and workers' compensation programs makes even less sense than it does under other labor-protective regimes,[176] especially in construction, where the formally self-employed "often work on multi-employer projects and, therefore, can affect the safety and health of other construction workers."[177]

The most startling revelation of the Census is that highway accidents and homicides were the leading causes of occupational injury-fatalities, accounting for 18 and 17 percent respectively of the total of 6,083 deaths.[178] More specifically, the Census found that highway accidents were the leading cause of death for male workers while homicides were the leading cause of death for women workers nationwide, for all workers in New York City, and for certain occupations such as taxi drivers.[179]

The data on female workers show that the traditional discrimination against and underrepresentation of women in such dangerous industries as construction, mining, agriculture, transportation, and even certain manufacturing occupations have largely spared them stereotypical industrial death and given a new dimension to *femme fatale*. This finding mirrors earlier research on nonfatal injuries that showed that although women who work in predominantly male occupations experienced injury rates similar to men's, their concentration in less dangerous occupations produced significantly lower overall injury rates.[180] If women accounted for only one percent of industrial fatalities in the United Kingdom at the turn of the century and only two percent in the United States in 1913,[181] by the time of the 1992 Census they still accounted for only 7 percent. Thus although there are almost as many women in the work force as men, the latter account for more than 13 times as many fatalities as the former. The 172 female homicide victims represented one-sixth of all murdered workers and two-fifths of all female fatalities, whereas the 254 women who died from non-homicidal injuries accounted for only 5 percent of such fatalities.[182] A similar pattern of gender-specific violence had already emerged from the NIOSH NTOF surveillance system during the 1980s. Of the 63,589 workers identified as having succumbed to fatal occupational injuries from 1980 to 1989, only 6 percent were women; of these women, 41 percent were victims of homicides compared to only 10 percent among men.[183]

Safety and Profit: Zero-Sum Game?

> As soon as the idea roots itself . . . that there are no industrial accidents, we shall begin to get full statistics of injuries. Working people speak of industrial injuries—they speak of murder. . . . Are we not foolish to talk of industrial accidents in a world governed by law, we who are all servants of modern science. . .? There is one . . . figure which serves to symbolize the statistics of industrial injuries to working people—the symbolic figure of Greed.[184]

These patterns create the impression that the hazards of the workplace merely reflect those of an increasingly and randomly dangerous world at large.[185] Indeed, homicides at work may, ironically, seem even more random that non-workplace homicides since most of the latter are committed by family members or acquaintances and relatively few in association with the commission of another felony, whereas most workplace homicides are committed by strangers in connection with robberies.[186] Media interpretation of such findings is continuous with the tradition that tends to view the place of employment not as a crucible of antagonistic class relationships but as a locus of societally indifferent individualized human interest stories.[187]

These phenomena and the sudden prominence that the news media, which otherwise devote little space to run-of-the-mill non-mass industrial fatalities, have conferred on them divert attention from the failure of the existing political-economic system to impose on firms liability costs in excess of injury prevention costs[188] or to incarcerate employers whose operations cause mass fatalities. Thus in 1988, after 18 years of OSHA and an additional 200,000 fatalities (as estimated by the NSC), the House Committee on Government Operations published a report entitled, *Getting Away with Murder in the Workplace: OSHA's Nonuse of Criminal Penal-*

ties for Safety Violations.[189] Even though "[t]he penalty for removing a tag from a mattress is higher than"[190] the weak criminal sanctions under OSHA against employers whose willful violation of a standard causes an employee's death,[191] "[n]o jail term ha[d] ever been meted out in a criminal case arising from an OSHA investigation into the death of a worker."[192] Not until 1989 did the first and only employer serve time (45 days) in prison for violating OSHA.[193]

Overall a sea change in discourse has taken place in the quarter-century since OSHA's enactment, when legislative advocates stressed the NSC's estimates of 140,000 industrial fatalities during the 1960s in order to conjure up images of satanic mills.[194] With the shift in employment away from the primary and secondary sectors of material production—only one-third of Census fatalities in 1992 occurred at industrial places, in mines, or on farms[195]—to the tertiary sector comprising less manual, bureaucratic service work, where the bulk of workplace homicides are committed, public attention is no longer directed to the thousands of construction workers who are "electrocuted, buried alive, crushed, or fall to their death"[196] or to the laborers whose accumulated lifetime of exposure to unhealthful conditions has led to an average age of death of 62.[197] Instead, the press concentrates on NIOSH alerts concerning the homicidal risk exposure of those who work alone exchanging money with the public at night in high-crime areas.[198]

This much more diffuse etiology deflects attention from the divergence between social and private costs, which underlies firms' failure to take adequate safety precautions.[199] One particularly poignant example of such profit-maximizing and injury-inducing entrepreneurial strategies is the expansion of output and reduction of unit costs through imposition of overtime and speed-ups on unskilled, low-paid workers, who then become fatigued.[200] In construction, today even more so than in the 1920s, "[m]oney and work schedules drive the industry so there's still an attitude that work must be completed quickly even if it means taking safety short-cuts."[201] Consequently, in an industry which does not yet subscribe to the view that "occupational injury and diseases are no longer considered to be the inevitable tribute to progress,"[202] "overexertion" is still the leading cause of accidents in private-sector construction,[203] and more than one-fifth of construction laborers cite the "fast pace of work" as a factor contributing to the injuries that they sustain.[204]

Remarkably, whereas one-quarter of private sector construction injuries are caused by overexertion, on work performed for the U.S. Army Corps of Engineers, where the aggregate accident rate is much lower, the corresponding share is only one-tenth.[205] Nor is this superior government safety record unusual: the "extensive safety program" developed by the

Tennessee Valley Authority in the 1930s, for example, also enabled it to achieve a rate of disabling injuries only one-sixth that of private firms.[206]

A basis for such different approaches to safety by the state and the for-profit sector has been set forth by a leading labor economist who nevertheless denied that "the capitalistic system" is to blame for industrial accidents because the profit motive is fed by what consumers want "or can be made to want." Although under socialism production would still take place in hazardous factories, he conceded one "important" difference—

> that the state, having substituted group welfare for the individual . . . profits motive, takes an even longer view than the far-sighted capitalistic employer: the state can make the prevention of accidents a vital part of group welfare rather than merely good business and, not being under the duress of competition, need not sacrifice its ideals for the demands of any immediate situation. In short, human values would be paramount.[207]

A comparison between socialist East and capitalist West Germany provided the most striking test and corroboration of this claim. Confirming that the latter's industrial injury rate was twice the former's, a West German government commission in 1971 explained the difference by reference to the superior system of labor protective controls in East Germany based in large part on the joint participation of unions and works councils.[208]

The same point was made negatively by the head of a captive (that is, steel company-owned) mining operation in explaining his commerical competitors' much higher fatality rates: "'If your stockholders expect to get a certain return, you've got to get it. And therefore you've got to be content with less safety if you're going to get more profit.'"[209] And as the vice president of a construction company and president of the National Constructors Association, an organization of the largest U.S. industrial construction firms, obliquely captured his competitors' reluctance to divert accumulatable profits into expenditures that might spare their workers maiming or death: "Contractors, by the very nature of their work, are cost-conscious, but their approach to savings is paradoxical. When compiling an estimate of cost, safety protection costs are often arbitrarily cut in an endeavor to be low bidder."[210]

The new focus on such firm-external injury sources as murderers and drunken drivers also abstracts from the empirically verified impact of the business cycle on injuries. The periodic hurling of inexperienced workers into and their expulsion from production—which unemployment then deprives them of the continuous experience that forms the best workers—are peculiarities of capitalism. The enormous increase in injury rates during World War II, for example, was in part a product of the unprecedented long-term unemployment of the Great Depression.[211] Nonfatal injuries, relatively few of which are caused by highway accidents or assaults, have retained a much more pronounced cyclical character.[212]

Conjunctural impacts on construction injuries take on a special form. Because industry practice has not been to include in bids a sum for safety and health measures, the International Labour Office has observed, "in times of recession there is a temptation to provide in the tender for methods of work that are cheaper but less safe. . . . The temptation is even greater when the cost of proper precautions is high in relation to the value of the job."[213] Since, from the workers' perspective, "'job security is more important than job safety'" during recessions, according to an OSHAdm inspector, "'workers don't ask questions when a foreman tells them to do something that might be dangerous.'"[214] The resulting rise in injuries may be concealed by the circumstance that workers may keep working during such periods of high unemployment for fear that employers will replace them with sturdier members of the reserve army.[215]

During upswings, in contrast, speedups, the exhaustion of the supply of skilled workers, and the hiring of less experienced workers lead to higher injury rates.[216] This cyclical structure assumes a special profile in construction with its disproportionately large sector of small, interest-sensitive firms compelled to complete contracts as quickly as possible in order to reduce loans charges, greater (and to some extent irrational) seasonality[217] and crowding of projects into short periods, and reliance on discrete projects. One extreme manifestation of the transiency of construction is the fact that three-quarters of injured construction laborers have less than one year's experience and one-eighth of all injuries to these workers take place on their first day at work, while one-quarter of all construction injuries occur during the worker's first month on the job.[218]

Counting on OSHA

In some states, there are far more game wardens than there are work safety inspectors. This had led some to observe that perhaps after all, safety is "for the birds."[219]

The issue of the extent and trend of industrial fatalities played an important part in the struggles for state intervention beginning in the late 1960s. "[T]he most important single factor" that prompted congressional action on OSHA "[p]robably . . . was the observed increase in the industrial accident rate, which rose nearly 29% from 1961 to 1970."[220] Such statistics are, however, too dry and barren to mobilize the political process. But then: "Good empirical studies are neither necessary nor sufficient

for the evolution of good policy. Sensational reports about tragic events
. . . are often more effective in eliciting legislative action."[221] Although
two-thirds of mine deaths occur individually in solitary "accidents" such
as roof falls, the fact that explosions and fires also kill large numbers of
workers at one time creates the kind of mass suffering qua human interest
story that compels news media to publicize the dangerous work, cavalier
business attitudes, and lackadaisical government enforcement. Thus the
deaths of 78 miners in the very modern Consolidation Coal Company
mine in Farmington, West Virginia in 1968 galvanized public opinion
long enough to pass the Federal Coal Mine Health and Safety Act of
1969;[222] the 91 miners who were killed in the Sunshine silver mine in
Idaho in 1972 focused the congressional mind sufficiently to amend that
statute in 1977 to include all mines.[223]

Largely deprived of the sympathy that the non-subterranean population periodically displays towards those whose life-chances have forced
them into their otherworldly fossorial work, the rest of the working class
faced significant political-economic and propagandistic obstacles to its efforts to impose legal restrictions on employers' control of the workplace.
These barriers emerged clearly during the run-up to the enactment of
OSHA. Resistance by the state to demands for intervention into managerial prerogatives was not new.[224] Prior to 1970, the federal government's
occupational safety and health private-sector jurisdiction applied to workers in plants with federal contracts as well as to longshore and harbor
workers.[225] Yet as a result of "[t]he Government's long-standing distaste
for a stronger, more aggressive enforcement policy . . . the available penalties [we]re almost never invoked against corporate offenders."[226]

At the same time, advocates of state intervention had to contend with
the disproportionality between media reporting on strikes and accidents,
especially in the construction industry. Injuries had "cost the industry"
17 million man-days annually between 1958 and 1965 whereas work stoppages resulted in only 3.8 million lost man-days;[227] indeed, in 1967 construction workers alone sustained disabling injuries resulting in almost as
many days lost as days lost to work stoppages in all industries.[228] If,
however, the president of the Building and Construction Trades Department of the AFL-CIO testified to Congress, the figures were reversed:

> The story would be spread over the front pages of the world. Loud demands
> would follow that the labor leaders involved in the stoppages be called to
> account. Public opinion would be outraged. On the other hand, accidents
> which result in millions of man-days lost—not to mention the human suffer-
> ing involved—generally are tucked away on the back pages to be eventu-
> ally ignored.[229]

Even the enactment and implementation of OSHA have failed to dissolve employers' resistance to systemic change. The corporate safety movement and construction firms in particular continue to insist that injuries are largely the result of human, that is, the workers' own fault.[230] "[T]he only way to make improvements in safety in construction," the chairman of the legislative committee of the Associated General Contractors of America explained to Congress, "is to educate the individual to operate on a safe basis."[231] Where, however, employers impose piece rates, which make workers "reluctant to use safety devices . . . for fear of slowing their production and cutting their pay checks,"[232] the injunction to operate safely might come with more grace from someone other than the employer who set those rates.[233]

This individualizing, blame-the-victim approach takes on an added dimension when a leader of the antiunion wing of the construction industry safety organization analogizes the victims to naughty children whose parent-employers are unfairly held legally responsible for their carelessness:

> [I]t's similar to dealing with children. If you tell them, go play and don't get close to the river. When they get too close, you have to do something. But they are personally held accountable.
>
> When they are in school and you have a test, the teacher says look, we're going to have a test tomorrow, you need to study this and study this, and some of them study it and they get good grades and some others don't study and they don't get good grades, but they are individually and personally held accountable.[234]

Construction unions have accommodated this programmatic infantilization of the working class by failing to vindicate an autonomous role for workers in creating safer working conditions than have traditionally been compatible with profitability. Instead, for example, the president of the United Brotherhood of Carpenters chose to combat management's line by pushing employers to exercise their panoply of managerial prerogatives vis-à-vis a passively compliant labor force:

> The employer sets the tone. If he refuses to tolerate unsafe work from workers who have been trained and warned about unsafe practices, then fires them if they continue to work unsafely, every other man and woman on the job will get the message and work safely. It's a simple proposition—you lose your job job if you don't listen to the boss.[235]

The dangers inherent in according employers a monopoly over safety emerge clearly from their own reaction to a proposed amendment to OSHA that would require construction employers to appoint a project safety coordinator to enforce a statutorily required health and safety plan to protect workers on each project.[236] When asked by a legislator why construction firms could not appoint their foremen as safety coordinators, the president of one firm, who also represented the National Association of Home Builders, responded that: "That will not work. . . . The reason is that the foreman has a conflict of interest. . . . The foreman's job is to make sure that the work is done on a specific schedule." While conceding that the foreman's job always involved "safety too," the employers' representative complained "that if we said to the foreman, you are the safety coordinator but . . . also part of your job is to get this particular application completed by a certain . . . time, when he sees a specific problem, is he going to look at the safety issue or is he going to look at his time schedule?"[237] Here the contradiction between human needs and the requirements of self-expanding value is at its sharpest.

The continuing high level and rate of fatalities and nonfatal injuries in construction, most of which even industry representatives admit are preventable,[238] is in part a function of the below-average provisioning by building firms of on-site doctors.[239] Although OSHA mandates safe workplaces,[240] the statute itself does not require employers to provide on-site physicians, nurses, or industrial hygienists. Instead, under OSHA regulations:

> (a) The employer shall ensure the ready availability of medical personnel for advice and consultation on matters of plant health.
> (b) In the absence of an infirmary, clinic, or hospital in near proximity to the workplace which is used for the treatment of all injured employees, a person or persons shall be adequately trained to render first aid.[241]

Regulations under OSHA and the Contract Work Hours and Safety Standards Act (which covers federal public works)[242] specifically tailored to the construction industry add that:

> (b) Provision shall be made prior to the commencement of the project for prompt medical attention in case of serious injury.
> (c) In the absence of an infirmary, clinic, hospital, or physician, that is reasonably accessible in terms of time and distance ot the worksite, which is available for the treatment of injured employees, a person who has a valid certificate license in first-aid training . . . shall be available at the worksite to render first aid.[243]

Construction firms in fact employ proportionally far fewer doctors and nurses than firms in general. In part this underrepresentation may be a function of the disproportionate weight of small firms in the industry.

Overall in the mid-1970s, 81 percent of all U.S. firms with more than 50,000 employees employed at least one full-time doctor compared to only 3 percent of those with fewer than 1,000 employees.[244] In 1972 the OSHAdm and NIOSH conducted the first survey of medical services provided by employers. In contrast to 21 percent of all private nonfarm and 69 percent of all manufacturing employees, only 1.5 percent of construction employees worked in establishments providing nurses' services. Similarly, only one in 13 construction employees worked in an establishment served by a doctor full time or part time compared to 26 percent of all private nonfarm and 36 percent of manufacturing employees. Moreover, only one construction employee in 14 worked in establishments providing the services of an industrial hygienist—who is qualified "to identify, measure, and evaluate health hazards in the work environment and to plan measures to eliminate, control, or reduce such hazards"— compared to 18 percent of all private nonfarm and 36 percent of manufacturing employees.[245] Finally, a more recent OSHAdm survey reveals that only one-sixth of all construction employees worked in firms that provide physical exams and medical tests to detect injuries and illnesses potentially related to work activities compared to one-third of all employees and three-fifths of all those employed in manufacturing.[246]

Finding no mathematical correlation between injury rates and the degree of provision of medical services among industry divisions, the BLS concluded "that the availability of nurses' services did not appear to be related to injury and illness experience."[247] Presumably the correlation in question is that between a high injury rate and a low degree of provision of medical services—as it exists, for example, in construction. Such a tangible causal chain would make plausible the conclusion that increasing such services would contribute to the reduction of injuries. In the more socially oriented societies of Western Europe, the starting point is inverted: there the initial hypothesis is that branches with high injury rates are precisely the ones that should also be well provided with medical services.[248]

Health and safety workers can, to be sure, prevent numerous injuries, mitigate the severity of others, and reduce fatalities through life-saving emergency services (as has also increasingly become the case on the military battlefield).[249] Since these services are provided by individual firms rather than by the state, risks may merely be shifted such that some workers must seek employment in firms that cannot afford such selectivity. What such intervention does not achieve, however, is elimination of the objective causes of injuries that inhere in a profit-driven competitive system. Such causes should not be confused with so-called technical defects, which are nothing but economic decisions made at a previous stage of production.[250]

Is It Worth Getting Killed at Work?

You never balance the wage against the risk; you balance the wage against the alternative. And the alternative is starving when you're put in this situation. That's what so phony about this cost/benefit analysis. A worker in the plant doesn't say, "Well, I'm getting $6.50 an hour so I'm gonna take this risk." The worker says, "I'm getting $6.50 an hour. If I open my mouth I might get nothing an hour, or I might get minimum wage. In that case, I can't afford to live." So, what's the difference? There's no difference for a person in that position. Either way they're trapped.[251]

One of the uses to which economists and public policy analysts have put industrial fatality data is to test whether labor markets provide a private consensual mechanism for achieving the socially "optimal amount of accident risk exposure" so as to maximize the difference between total benefits—unimpeded production creating wages for workers, profits for firms, and products for consumers—and costs—purportedly including the physical, mental, and economic costs to workers.[252] Perfectly competitive labor markets are said to create incentives for firms, which are assumed to internalize all accident costs, to take measures to reduce injury levels sufficiently to be able to recruit workers with as small a wage premium as possible.[253]

Thus, according to the original version of this thesis, Adam Smith's doctrine of compensatory wages, if an industry, such as construction, is extraordinarily hazardous, its workers will be indemnified for the uncommon risks to which they are exposed: "The wages of labour vary with the ease or hardship, the cleanliness or dirtiness, the honourableness or dishonourableness of the employment." This tendency to equality of the "whole of the advantages and disadvantages of the different employments" presupposed, to be sure, that "every man was perfectly free both to chuse what occupation he thought proper, and to change it as often as he thought proper."[254]

Smith assumed, in other words, that workers do not knowingly accept unsafe employment without some offsetting benefit such as a wage higher than that associated with a less unsafe job. Smith did not credit the possibility that some workers might be constrained to perform dangerous work without additional compensation simply because the alternative was that they and their family would "'all starve together.'"[255] Nor could his model accommodate the possibility that workers tolerated unsafe workplaces for fear that they might lose their livelihood. An incident in Britain in the 1980s presented the starkest imaginable illustration of this pressure: the parents of a seventeen-year-old worker whose arm had been trapped in a machine not only promised to waive compensation, but even to pay for the damage to the machine—if only their son could retain his job.[256]

With alacrity nineteenth-century Anglo-American courts adopted the Smithian fiction of free and equal contracting between atomized labor and aggregated capital in adjudicating workers' personal injury claims against their employers. In the first U.S. case testing and denying an employer's liability for such negligence,[257] a concurring judge asserted in 1841 that: "No prudent man would engage in any perilous employment, unless seduced by greater wages than he could earn in a pursuit unattended by any unusual danger."[258] And the following year, in a decision that would reverberate to workers' detriment into the next century, Chief Justice Shaw of the Massachusetts Supreme Judicial Court held that a worker employed to perform specified services "takes upon himself the natural and ordinary risks and perils incident to the performance of such services, and in legal presumption, the compensation is adjusted accordingly."[259]

Yet neither the judiciary nor the economics profession was hermetically impervious to a more realistic analysis of the allegedly free occupational choices made by the working class. While granting that Smith's conclusions followed from his premises, John Stuart Mill found the real world of the 1850s staggeringly different from the one that Smith had conjured up. In an economy permanently shaped by widespread unemployment:

> The really exhausting and . . . repulsive labours, instead of being better paid than others, are almost invariably paid the worst of all, because performed by those who have no choice. It would be otherwise in a favourable state of the general labour market. . . . But when the supply of labour so far exceeds the demand that to find employment at all is an uncertainty, and to be offered it on any terms a favour, the case is totally the reverse. . . . The more revolting the occupation, the more certain it is to receive the minimum of remuneration, because it devolves on the most helpless and degraded. . . . [T]he inequalities of wages are generally in an opposite direction to the equitable principle of compensation erroneously represented by Adam Smith as the general law of the remuneration of labour. The hardships and the earnings, instead of being directly proportional, as in any just arrangements of society they would be, are generally in an inverse ratio to one another.[260]

Nor was Mill alone in this heterodox view. Even as conservative an institution as the British High Court pierced the Smithian fiction as early as 1888. In ruling in favor of a carpenter who had sued an employer for negligently causing his workplace injury, the court offered a model of legal realism: "If the plaintiff could have gone away from the dangerous place without incurring the risk of losing his means of livelihood, the case might have been different; but he was obliged to be there; his poverty, not his will, consented to incur the damage."[261]

About the same time, Alfred Marshall, Mill's successor as the English-speaking world's foremost economist, advanced a variant of this particular attack on the Smithian presumption—albeit from a social Darwinian viewpoint.[262] Equalizing differences were inapplicable to

> the disagreeableness of work . . . if it is of such a kind that it can be done by those whose industrial abilities are of a very low order. For the progress of science has kept alive many people who are unfit for any but the lowest grade of work. They compete eagerly for the comparatively small quantity of work for which they are fitted, and in their urgent need they think almost exclusively of the wages they can earn: they cannot afford to pay much attention to incidental discomforts. . . .
>
> Hence arises the paradoxical result that the dirtiness of some occupations is a cause of the lowness of the wages earned in them. For employers find that this dirtiness adds much to the wages they would have to pay to get the work done by skilled men of high character working with improved appliances; and so they often adhere to old methods which require only unskilled workers of but indifferent character, and who can be hired for low . . . wages, because they are not worth much to any employer.[263]

The belated clamor for workers' compensation legislation in the United States during the first decade of the twentieth century brought in its wake a fresh onslaught on Smithianism emanating from the highest office. In a special message to Congress, President Theodore Roosevelt himself observed that: "In theory, if wages were always freely and fairly adjusted, they would always include an allowance as against the risk of injury, just as certainly as the rate of interest for money includes an allowance for insurance against the risk of loss." In fact, however, the workers' world did not work that way.[264] P. Tecumseh Sherman, the legal expert of the influential pro-corporate National Civic Federation, testifying before the New York State Commission on Employers Liability, went even farther: "These people are not free to leave these hazardous employments and to go to non-hazardous employments. As a mass they are bound by necessity to the work. [T]here is no free assumption; it is forced assumption."[265] And that commission itself recommended enactment of a workers' compensation program because "the laissez faire system of political economy . . . does not work out."[266]

Such anti-Smithian arguments have, however, fallen out of favor. Contemporary orthodox economists may concede that wages are formed differently than other commodity prices[267] but nevertheless adhere to the mechanistic notion of "equalizing differences."[268] According to W. Kip Viscusi, the theory's chief academic proponent in the industrial injury context, the Smithian claim "that individuals require higher wages to accept jobs they view as hazardous" hinges on two minimal prerequisites: "that workers prefer being healthy to being dead or injured and that they prefer more consumption to less."[269]

Contrary to Viscusi's assertion, however, the model of perfect competition underlying the doctrine of equalizing differences implicitly assumes a much broader array of worker characteristics and a set of employer-employee relationships that are far from typical: equal bargaining power, infinite mobility, and encyclopedic information.[270] In contemporary econometric modeling, like nineteenth-century judicial opinions, "[t]he economic compulsion which left [the worker] no choice except starvation, or equally dangerous employment elsewhere, [i]s entirely disregarded."[271] Thus, for example, workers who are considerably more disadvantaged by their employer's power or right to fire them at-will than the employer is discomfited by their freedom to quit are hardly in a position to demand the elimination of unsafe working conditions.

Attempts by those late-twentieth-century economists who bother to take note of Mill's "paradox that the most attractive jobs in society are also the highest paid" to reconcile it with Smith's notion of compensatory wages reinforce rather than undermines Mill's position. Thus again according to Viscusi:

> a worker with greater wealth will be less willing to incur job risks or . . . the premium necessary to induce him to accept any particular risk will be greater.
>
> This behavior is similar to many other patterns of consumer choice. Richer consumers purchase better cuts of meat, more comprehensive health insurance, and higher-quality cars. The influence of a worker's wealth on his willingness to incur an occupational risk arises from a similar variation in tastes. . . . Individuals at the top of the occupational hierarchy . . . have a wider range of work opportunities. Their more affluent economic status will be reflected in a lower willingness to boost their income even further through work on a hazardous job. . . . [272]

Instead of resolving the alleged paradox, Viscusi has merely rephrased Mill's theory of noncompeting groups: workers without choices are compelled to submit to fatal risks that others are in a position to avoid. When, in addition, employers in particularly unsafe industries reorganize production processes in order to replace skilled workers (who have choices) with less skilled workers, who have fewer opportunities to avoid hazardous employment, firms can recruit a labor force without offering any significant premia.[273]

Because the absence of the Smithian prerequisites has historically made the doctrine of compensatory wages unrealistic, early advocates of workers' compensation programs took the position that: "This legal fiction . . . has no basis in fact; railroad trainmen, for instance, obtain no more than the wages of ordinary laborers, although one out of every eleven of them is seriously injured every year. [O]ther workmen in extrahazardous trades are paid no more than laborers in other occupations, excepting where the matter of skill enters into the question."[274] Another proponent of state intervention even charged that "dangerous trades really pay lower rather than higher wages, or, stated in another form, such industries command the services of only the poorly paid laborers."[275] Recent econometric studies confirm the absence of statistical significance between wage rates and occupational death rates.[276] And even Viscusi is constrained to conclude from his empirical study that "blue-collar workers in the more hazardous occupations do not receive additional remuneration that is sufficiently great to be visible to the casual observer."[277] Risk premia for fatal injuries that have been calculated in the range of a few percentage points[278] cannot support the claim that the labor market fully compensates such workers for the risks to which their employer exposes them.[279] Even state intervention in the form of workers' compensation programs fails to close the gap—especially in states where they provide poverty-level replacement benefits far below the worker's average income or exclude whole groups of workers such as agricultural workers, who are exposed to extraordinary risks.[280]

Recent surveys cast further doubt on the Smithian dogma by showing that, although workers with tenure of one to three months incurred three times as many injuries as those with one to three years tenure and eight times as many injuries as those with more than twenty years tenure, fewer than 30 percent of beginners reported severe hazards to management compared to 70 percent of workers who had been at a place of employment between five and ten years.[281] As a chemical worker, for example, who expressed great trepidation about the "white, drippy, slimy stuff . . . hanging all over" him as a result of being required to work in a lime kiln, remarked: "Most guys won't tell their foreman, 'I'm not going to do it,' because they just got hired and they'll lose their job. . . . We don't really have a choice. I can't refuse to work knowing that tomorrow I can get another job. I can't look for a year and a half for a job. I'd lose everything."[282]

As OSHA was going into effect in 1971, several dozen *Wall Street Journal* reporters inadvertently launched an impressive assault on the doctrine of equalizing differences while examining the question as to why a worker would "continue to work at a job that has cost him his health and paid him a wage that he has had to struggle on all his grown life." In the course of discovering that "Brutal, Mindless Labor Remains a Daily Reality for Millions in the U.S.," the journalists kept hearing the same answer: "'There aren't many jobs around here for a high school dropout. . . . I'd leave in a minute, but where would I go?' That is the dilemma of millions of relatively unskilled laborers. . . . They mine coal, shovel steel slag, gut animal carcasses." Asked why he tended iron melting furnaces in 140° heat, another worker responded that "[t]here's only three choices—work, starve, or go to jail." Although coke oven workers "exhibit considerable militancy about pollution and safety . . . the men know that, in the end, the company has the upper hand. 'As long as the company can get another man to take your job if you go home, they'll do nothing.'" Why did coke oven workers at a U.S. Steel Corporation plant who walked under walls of flames and on bricks as hot as 180° and inhaled such quantities of toxins that they were "ten times more likely to die of lung cancer than the average steelworker," nevertheless receive "a low wage for a steelworker"? This particular anti-Smithian outcome may have been overdetermined by the racially discriminatory assignment of an overwhelmingly black work force to this uncompensatedly life-threatening work.[283] This aspect of racism, far from being confined to a few plants, is a statistically significant macroeconomic phenomenon.[284]

The finding that union workers secure higher risk premia for hazardous jobs than do atomized workers casts additional doubt on the "'adequacy' of the nonunion market."[285] Unless they are employed in highly unionized industries, "[w]orkers in very hazardous occupations . . . do not receive meaningful levels of hazard pay."[286] Indeed, several studies have even shown negative compensating wage differentials for nonunion workers exposed to fatal hazards.[287] This divergence results from differences not only in bargaining power but also in knowledge: a union with thousands of members knows that a certain have been and will be injured every year whereas an individual worker may underestimate her risk level by generalizing from limited experience.[288]

A comparison of unionized and nonunionzed construction and non-construction laborers will illustrate this point. Construction laborers are exposed to one of the highest occupational fatality rates in the United States. From 1980 to 1989, 39.5 per 100,000 of them were killed on the job compared to about 17 among non-construction laborers; during the same period, the corresponding rates for all construction workers and all workers were 25.6 and 7.0 respectively.[289] For 1992, the Census of Fatal Occupational Injuries revealed a 3 to 1 ratio in fatality rates between construction and non-construction laborers.[290] A study of unprecedented detail conducted by the BLS shed light on union-nonunion wage differentials in 1970. Among year-round, full-time construction laborers, 34 percent of whom were unionized, unionists' median annual earnings were 70 percent greater than those of their nonunion counterparts.[291] Among non-construction laborers, 46 percent of whom were organized, the union premium was 48 percent.[292] Among unionists, construction laborers' earnings were 13 percent greater than those of their non-construction counterparts, whereas those of nonunionists in construction were actually 1 percent lower than their non-construction counterparts.[293] Nonunion construction laborers thus received no additional compensation for subjecting themselves to a significantly higher risk of being killed on the job than their non-construction counterparts. Although unionized construction laborers were able to extract a greater premium vis-à-vis their non-union competitors than any other occupational group, their premium over the wages of their non-construction counterparts, who face a much smaller chance of being killed, is modest.

Modified surveys for 1977 and 1980 compared mean weekly earnings of full-time workers who were and were not represented by labor organizations (the data for 1980 are in parentheses). The earnings premium of the 40 (47) percent of construction laborers who were represented was 55 (34) percent vis-à-vis the unrepresented; among non-construction laborers the corresponding figures were 46 (45) percent and 50 (44) percent. Represented construction laborers' earnings were only 12 (7) percent higher than those of their non-construction counterparts, whereas among the unrepresented the premium was 8 (16) percent.[294] By the end of the 1970s, organized construction laborers' earnings premium vis-à-vis the unorganized not only shrank, but ceased to be an outlier.

Recent empirical psychological experiments have further undermined the plausibility of the Smithian compensation doctrine. The crucial concept here is the disparity between the willingness to buy and the willingness to sell or accept an entitlement.[295] Consider a worker whose weekly wage is $300 and faces a 1 in 1,000 risk of being injured. When asked by her employer, who controls the workplace and thus owns the entitlement in question, how much she would be willing to pay the employer to introduce changes that would reduce that risk to 1 in 10,000, she offers $30. Now consider the (counterfactual) case in which the worker owns the entitlement and the employer must secure the worker's consent to changes in the process of production that would bring about an increase in injury risk from 1 in 10,000 to 1 in 1,000. Extrapolation from analogous experiments suggests that the smallest bribe that the worker would demand might be more than one order of magnitude larger than the largest amount she is willing to pay for a proportionate increase in safety.[296] The first survey of willingness to exchange money for increases or decreases in workplace fatal accident risks, though methodologically biased toward underestimation, nevertheless found that respondents demanded almost three times as much in annual wage increases to accept an increment in risk as the wage that they would forego to obtain a decrement of the same magnitude.[297]

This kind of disparity between willingness to pay and willingness to sell is driven by several forces. First, although universal marketization and the comcomitant formation of a market price may induce people to value fungible commodities more or less identically whether they are buying or selling, this tendency vanishes with regard to a unique, nonreproducible good such as health and safety. Here people "are usually willing to sell the right to be free from increased mortality risks for considerably more than they are willing to pay for reduced mortality risks." Thus a second way of explaining the disparity is that contrary to Coase's theorem, which assumes that outcomes are independent of the initial assignment of the entitlement as between buyer and seller, "most of us can demand much more in a bargain in which we are asked to sacrifice something of great value to which we have a 'right' than we can afford to pay for that same thing if someone else has the right to take it from us."[298]

Finally, disparity between buying and selling valuations also results from the diminishing marginal utility of income and/or the asymmetrical valuation that market participants attach to losing already realized income and receiving additional income. Consequently, losing income equal to 10 percent of a given standard of living diminishes satisfaction considerably more than a 10 percent rise in income would increase satisfaction. Thus if workers whose existing budgets exhaust their income were required to buy safety entitlements with income they already have, but had to sell such entitlements for additions to current income, it is plausible that the price at which they would be willing to sell would exceed that at which they would buy.[299]

Since all wage-premium studies are implicitly based on the real-capitalist premise that the employer owns the entitlement,[300] they must significantly understate the premium that would result from a system in which workers held workplace safety and health entitlements and employers were the supplicants. Consequently, "the economic positivist's methodological insistence on propositions that can be tested creates a strong bias, not merely in favor of markets, but also in favor of the status quo assignment of entitlements."[301] To be sure, in a full-employment economy workers might hold a market-based entitlement to avoid dangerous jobs such that competition for labor would compel employers either to improve working conditions or to raise wages sufficiently to induce workers to sell that right.[302] Absent such a transformation of capitalism, however, the pseudo-positivist fictional reconstruction of implicitly bargained-for compensating wage differentials not only atavistically resurrects the patently unrealistic and biased judicial doctrines of the pre-workers' compensation period, but also logically supports dismantling OSHA's incipient transformation of the fictitious industrial safety and health market into a nontransferable entitlement. President Reagan's Council of Economic Advisers, for example, adopted a position embodying all of these elements.[303]

Employers' cavalier and almost aggressive admission of the unreality of the Smithian assumption of a perfectly competitive labor market is tragicomic. Thus in congressional testimony reminiscent of the law's majestic equality in prohibiting both the rich and the poor from sleeping under bridges, the president of the Associated General Contractors of America (and future governor of Mississippi) was asked whether a construction worker who is asked by an unscrupulous employer to go into a ditch lacking supports has the right to refuse. Kirk Fordice replied: "Yes, sir, I certainly do. He has to risk his employment, I presume, in that situation. But certainly, any individual should have that right."[304]

In spite of this brazenly stripped-down version of freedom, which amounts to little more than the absence of slavery—and, in addition, misstates the law since, under certain exigent circumstances, workers are entitled to refuse to subject themselves to unsafe conditions although they may have to spend years vindicating that right[305]—construction is said to provide concrete historical examples of the Smithian compensatory mechanism. Thus according to Stanley Lebergott, a leading labor statistician and economic historian:

> [A] mighty influence buoying up wages paid to the men building canals during the 1820s and 1830s was the danger of yellow fever and malaria. Built through marsh and swamps . . . to reduce construction problems, the canals were known as killers. . . .
>
> In upstate New York in the 1830s and 1840s grown men received $10 to $12 for farm work, but thirteen-year-old boys driving an Erie canal boat through the region where hundreds died during the cholera season were paid as much. With boys customarily being paid markedly less than men, and certainly for less arduous work, the differential presumably reflected the dangers of cholera and malaria associated with being a "canawler." The allowance for unhealthy working conditions was a quite explicit part of entrepreneurial calculations.[306]

How a few dollars compensated a child for his failure to survive beyond the age of thirteen remains unclear.[307] It is this perspective, which regards work injuries not as a societal problem but "at most as an economic problem," that became incorporated in workers' compensation statutes.[308] As advocates of workers' compensation programs during the Progressive Era were wont to stress: "For the . . . delirium of terror in the fall through endless hollow squares of steel beams down to the death-delaying construction planks of the rising skyscraper . . . there can be no compensation."[309] Continuous with this emphasis on the inherently nonfungible, nonexchangeable, and noncompensable nature of physical and mental well-being is the reaction of (the adult children of) unionized miners. From an industry that perpetuated "the notion that the added production costs of available safety procedure were less acceptable than continued death" they demanded not additional compensation for exposing themselves to the risk of "never coming out" alive and thus joining the more than 100,000 miners who have been killed in this century, but safer conditions.[310]

In order to dull this insight into the incommensurability between life and money, "[a] discourse and institutional practices are needed to harmonize the [employer-employee] relationship so that the blood-money exchange can be conducted without calling into question the moral basis of the relationship within which the suffering was created."[311] In the latter part of the twentieth century, entrepreneurial opposition to state intervention such as OSHA has coalesced with a broader based ideology and practice of universal marketization to resurrect the requisite discourse. The Smithian model of perfect competition presupposes the absence of external economies such that each agent bears all the costs of its decisions.[312] Yet the failure of firms to internalize the entire economic— let alone social—cost of the injuries caused by their operations underscores the fundamental difference in the way capitalist economies and their legal systems treat the productive wear and tear of human beings on the one hand and the means of production on the other. In order to spread the cost of a large and risky investment in machines over as many product units as possible before that equipment becomes obsolete, firms have an incentive to operate them as quickly and as continuously as possible. "Capitalistic enterprise thus naturally tends toward a long working day and week. This, however . . . produces fatigue among employees."[313] To replace deteriorated assets and thus to maintain the value of their capital investment intact, firms include depreciation charges in their prices: "[N]o owner of durable factors of production would be willing to make use of such agents, if some provision were not made to compensate him for the deterioration of his asset."[314]

Why can human agents not make similar charges for their physical impairment? After all, as a commissioner of the California Industrial Accident Commission observed of the toll incurred in one of the early years of workers' compensation: "When we kill in industry 23,000 men we have wiped out a property value of the Nation."[315] Why is it that "[i]f instead of 20,000 workers, 20,000 head of cattle were exposed to certain death . . ., there would be an easily calculable incentive to adopt required preventive measures"?[316] Or as the United Brotherhood of Carpenters put it mechanistically: "The injured workman is just as much an incident of the modern factory, as is the damaged machine. Both are proper items of operating expense, and should come out of the employers' profits. The only capital of the employeee is his labor power."[317]

An historical example straddling capitalist and slave societies makes such "entrepreneurial calculations" easier to grasp: 600 Irish immigrants died annually in the 1830s digging the Pontchartrain canal in the "fever-racked swamps around New Orleans" in pursuit of sixty cents more an hour than railway construction near Philadelphia paid because no slave owner would consider permitting his $900-slave to perish for such a price.[318] Because the individual worker, as self-owned, lacks capital value,[319] her inferior bargaining position, especially in periods of high unemployment, makes it difficult for her to have her "claim to special financial compensation in case of hazardous occupations recognized by the entrepreneur."[320] Until society at large, by means of comprehensive intervention, imposes full internalization of social costs on firms and empowers workers to assume responsibility for their own health and safety by shaping their working conditions, employers will continue to have an economic incentive to economize on the use of their fixed capital by churning their labor force and replacing worn-out workers with as yet unimpaired ones.[321]

In a democratically organized society, complete injury data would enable workers and consumers to deliberate on what to produce and how to produce it in order to avoid or limit products created in production processes that according to society's conscious determination unduly infringe on producers' physical and mental integrity.[322] Accurate fatality statistics remain "good stuff" to start that revolution with too.

NOTES

Preface

1. KENNETH DAVIS, ADMINISTRATIVE LAW TEXT 4 (3d ed. 1972 [1951]).
2. *See, e.g.*, Kenneth Prewitt, *Public Statistics and Democratic Politics*, in THE POLITICS OF NUMBERS 261 (William Alonso & Paul Starr ed. 1987).
3. OSKAR MORGENSTERN, ON THE ACCURACY OF ECONOMIC OBSERVATIONS 10 (2d ed. 1965 [1950]).
4. PATRICIA COHEN, A CALCULATING PEOPLE: THE SPREAD OF NUMERACY IN EARLY AMERICA 211 (1982).
5. *See, e.g.*, Christopher Jenks, *The Politics of Income Measurement*, in The Politics of Numbers at 83, 126–31. For examples of methodological critiques that go further, see Margo Conk, *Occupational Classification in the United States Census: 1870–1940*, 9 J. INTERDISCIPLINARY HIST. 111 (1978); Victor Perlo, *The Fake Claims of Declining Productivity and Its Political Use*, 46 SCI. & SOC'Y 284 (1982); MARC LINDER, FAREWELL TO THE SELF-EMPLOYED: DECONSTRUCTING A SOCIOECONOMIC AND LEGAL SOLIPSISM (1992).

I. From Surplus Value to Unit Labor Costs

1. Pronounced as in the German, *Ulk* ("practical joke").
2. An unusual and oblique acknowledgment of such struggles can be found in advertisements by states and nations of the multiples that their workers "give back . . . in value added for every dollar they're paid" (*Business Week* 1974; Malabre 1976).
3. For a detailed discussion of the statistical-conceptual problems of gathering the underlying data, see Shelton & Chandler (1963a); Mark (1968).
4. There are also instances of secular declines in ULC such as that during the last quarter of the nineteenth century in Britain (Phelps Brown 1968, 126–29).
5. For an analysis of this scenario in terms of ULC, see Schultze (1959, 22).
6. Although the General Council wanted to print the debate between Marx and Weston, Marx never published it. On the one hand, he thought publication would be useful because some Council members had connections with John Stuart Mill; on the other hand, to have "'Mr. Weston' as opponent [is] not exactly very flattering" (Marx 1965, 125). Citizen Weston, in turn, did not feel that Marx had refuted any of his principles (Institute of Marxism-Leninism [1964], 109–12).
7. It is therefore a half-truth to adduce the AFL's adoption of the policy of tying wages to productivity as an example of conservatism (O'Connor 1986, 45).
8. Even the published text of Green's Declaration bears traces of its Germanic authorship. Thus, for example, the lack of the indefinite article in the phrase "higher productivity without corresponding increase of real wages" (Green 1927a, 919) makes the sentence ungrammatical English; its literal German counterpart, however, would be a component of a well-formed sentence ("höhere Produktivität ohne entsprechende Reallohnerhöhung").
9. When, four years later, Douglas did expressly discuss the relationship between increases in real wages and productivity, he used the Green-Kuczynski formulation of the issue as his point of departure (Douglas 1930, 504).
10. Kuczynski states that "it is well-known that after a single mention Marx had never again returned to the idea of relative wages" (Kuczynski 1973, 124). In fact, however, sixteen years after raising the issue, Marx did return to it in his talk to the General Council of the First International (Marx 1849, 413; Marx 1992, 178).
11. Contrary to Kuczynski's reconstruction forty-five years later, just a year earlier Kuczyn-

ski himself had appeared to doubt the reality of absolute immiseration while stressing the prevalence of the relative variant (Kuczynski 1926d, 127–28).

12. It is unclear why Kuczynski used the term "social wage," which in Europe had been applied to wages as supplemented by family allowances (Waggaman 1923; Waggaman 1924; Tarnow 1927).

13. When this book, which Kuczynski had written with his wife, was being translated into Russian, the galley proofs happened to be seen by Stalin, who, disturbed by the large number of errors, told old Bolshevik Karl Radek to write a foreword pointing them out. Having heard the story, the next time he was in Moscow Kuczynski rushed to Radek for the details. Before answering, however, Radek wanted to know which part Kuczynski had written and which his wife. Being a "gentleman," Kuczynski answered that of course she had written the good parts and he the bad. To which Radek replied: "Aha, Comrade Kuczynski, then that means that you wrote the book all by yourself!" (Kuczynski 1973, 176). Ironically the Kuczynskis also expressed their gratitude in this book to Thorne and Scattergood for "crucial instruction" (Kuczynski & Kuczynski 1930, iii).

14. According to one source, Kuczynski had already joined in 1925—before he left for the United States (Who's Who 1989, 2:640).

15. Labor's share in production for individual industries appears to be simply wages divided by value added. For industry as a whole, for which Kuczynski provided only index numbers, he used this formula: payroll/employment/(physical volume of production x wholesale prices of non-agricultural commodities)/population. To arrive at labor's share in consumption, Kuczynski substituted in the numerator of the denominator: (physical volume of production of food and textiles x retail prices of food and clothing) (Kuczynski 1928a, 327; Kuczynski & Steinfeld 1928, 830 n.1).

16. It also mistakenly referred to the author as "Jüsgen Viczynski" ("Labor's Share in Production" 1927).

17. See Aron (1962, 260–65); Wagner (1976, 13–99).

18. The Labor Research Association characterized the rate of surplus value and the worker's relative position as two different ways of analyzing labor's share of national product, but used different sources for the two calculations and failed to note that their quantitative movements were not mirror images of each other (Labor Research Association 1948, 47–55, 78–84, 97–99). Leading members of the CPUSA founded this organization in 1927 (Biographical Dictionary of the American Left 1986, 388; Encyclopedia of the American Left 1990, 347).

19. In a speech to the U.S. Senate on June 14, 1951, Joseph McCarthy said that it would be impossible to answer "the question of why we fell from our position as the most powerful Nation on earth at the end of World War II to a position of declared weakness by our leadership . . . without uncovering a conspiracy so immense and an infamy so black as to dwarf any previous such venture in the history of man" (U.S. Congress 1951, 6556).

20. Weintraub divided an index of factory payrolls by an index of physical volume of production; the result as multiplied by 100 produced an index of labor cost per unit of output. He then divided an index of hourly earnings by this index of labor cost to generate the output per man-hour index that he required to analyze unemployment.

21. Even a staunch opponent of the Fifth Amendment concedes that its invocation against "governmental snooping and oppression concerning political . . . beliefs . . . is the privilege we love" (Friendly 1968, 696).

22. The crisis of the mid-1970s, which afforded Marxist economists "a measure of attention . . . when many mainstream economists appear[ed] caught in an interpretive whirlpool," provided an ironic opportunity for Magdoff's re-emergence as an economic consultant. After appearing at a panel discussion with a corporation president, "Mr. Magdoff says, the businessman approached him and suggested the two get together privately to talk about the economy" (Newman 1975).

23. Several months before Perlo's article appeared, an anonymous article in the Monthly Labor Review summarizing Magdoff's study added less than two pages on ULC. It noted

that the strong drop in the 1920s had not been accompanied by a comparable increase in wages or lower prices ("Employment and Production" 1939, 1403–1404).

24. This approach is also rooted in the transformation of the value components of the commodity into autonomous sources of revenue. The empirical observation that a general increase in wages produces a decline in the rate of profit and changes production prices in accordance with the organic composition of capital in various industries induces the belief that prices rise because wages rise and conceals the "regulation of these changes by the value of commodities, which is independent of wages" (Marx 1964, 875).

25. Comparisons of AULC and unit nonlabor costs can also cast light on labor-capital income shifts (Herman & Fulco 1969, 13–14).

26. To the extent that the price deflators for manufacturing output diverge from those used for deflating compensation—that is to say, to the extent that the commodities entering into the consumption of the recipients of labor income are produced in other sectors—it is more appropriate to cast the underlying output and compensation data in current dollars. "Morever, an individual producer is not interested in the smallest degree in the level of real wages. He does not, in his business capacity, even enquire what it is" (Keynes 1979, 98). By the same token, calculation of RULC for a single industry is meaningless when the deflators or rates of productivity diverge widely between the industries producing commodities consumed by the working class and that single industry (Kaplan 1958 29–38, appendix tables 35–42).

27. For skepticism as to whether ULC analysis can provide evidence of causality from wages to prices, see White (1988).

28. For an analysis of income distribution using real wages as the point of comparison, see Bergmann, Jacobi, & Müller (1975, 107–15, 355).

29. For an example of a journalistic account that expressly refers to "nominal unit labor costs" and even emphasizes that "in real terms, employers now spend 3.8% less for pay . . . per unit of output, see Bernstein (1993, 120).

30. Whereas Raskin described the development of productivity in a purely objective fashion—"Output per man hour, the standard measure of productivity"—he stated that "union leaders . . . insist that their members have been badly short-changed as a result of the runaway climb of living costs in the last three years" (Raskin 1976).

31. For an example of Party-Marxist use of RULC, see Hemberger et al. (1968, 626).

32. As two of the prewar period's leading labor economists articulated the program: "Any generalized statement of the forces determining distribution in . . . capitalism should be based upon a knowledge not only of the trend of labor's real remuneration but also of whether there has been a gain or loss in comparison with the returns . . . to property and enterprise" (Millis & Montgomery 1938, 135).

33. Constant capital coefficients in connection with constant factor shares and rate of profit presuppose that capital intensity and "labor productivity" grow at the same rate.

34. The German counterpart to the Council of Economic Advisers, very attentive to the effect of the proletarianization of the self-employed on the distribution of income, regularly published adjusted figures for labor's share to take this shift into account (Sachverständigenrat 1972, 146–47).

35. For a similar Marxist critique, see Mandel (1971, 28–39).

36. For evidence that in lieu of an incomes policy, the Swedish labor unions' solidaristic wage policy fulfilled the same function, see Dencik (1974).

37. On Solow's awareness of the existence of a considerably wider range of shifts in "distributive shares," see Solow (1960, 95–103).

38. Although Menshikov's book was translated from the Russian, the publisher believes that it was probably never published in that language.

39. Menshikov separately proposed an incomes policy that would have prohibited firms from raising prices by the amount of the increase in their ULC (Menshikov 1975b).

40. In other words, the simplifying assumption that the general price index and the consumer price index coincide is unrealistic.

41. The issue of compensation of owners and their families can be eliminated by focusing on "the corporate sector where there is a definite distinction between labor and nonlabor payments" (Herman & Fulco 1969, 14).

42. In 1962 Perlo published a technical critique of one of the components of ULC—the index of industrial production (Perlo 1962).

43. For similar calculations (presumably done by Perlo) for an industry, see Communist Party (1970, 18–22).

44. Perlo later adopted a more nuanced view (Perlo 1988, 27–30).

45. Although some conceptual flaws marred the real spendable average weekly earnings series, its critics seemed chiefly irritated by the fact that the average had been lowered since the 1960s by the enormous influx of low-paid women and teenagers (Perry 1972; National Commission on Employment and Unemployment Statistics 1979, 206–208; Moore 1980, 182–91; Flaim 1982; U.S. BLS 1983, 204–206).

46. Historical amnesia had apparently so enveloped the subject that the editors of *World Marxist Review* found it necessary to append a footnote to Perlo's article speculating that by "relative wages" he "probably means the share sof wages in the national income" (Perlo 1990a, 83 n.4).

47. President Carter's Council of Economic Advisers, the chairman of which was Charles Schultze, did discuss the shares of corporate profits and employee compensation in its *Annual Report* (U.S. Council 1979, 26–27; U.S. Council 1980, 40–41; U.S. Council 1981, 155).

II. Fatal Subtraction

1. Crystal Eastman, *The Three Essentials for Accident Prevention*, 38 ANNALS AM. ACAD. POL. & SOC. SCI. 98, 99 (1911).

2. A total of 938,400 fatalities has been estimated for the years 1928 through 1992. Calculated according to data in NATIONAL SAFETY COUNCIL, ACCIDENT FACTS 1993 EDITION 26–27 (1993). For the mid-1920s, the managing director of the same organization estimated average annual industrial fatalities at 23,000. W. Cameron, *Organizing for Safety Nationally*, ANNALS, Jan. 1926, at 27, 30.

3. Pub. L. No. 91–956, § 5(a), 84 Stat. 1590, 1593 (1970) (codified at 29 U.S.C. § 654(a)(1) (1988)).

4. § 24(a), 84 Stat. at 1614 (codified at 29 U.S.C. § 673(a)).

5. *OSHA Injury and Illness Information System: Hearing Before a Subcomm. of the House Comm. on Government Operations*, 98th Cong, 2d Sess. 33 (1984) (testimony of Karl Kronebusch, U.S. Office of Technology Assessment). Estimates range from 10,000 to 210,000.

6. Guy Toscano & Janice Windau, *Fatal Work Injuries: Results from the 1992 National Census*, MONTHLY LABOR REVIEW, Oct. 1993, at 39, 42; COUNTING INJURIES AND ILLNESSES IN THE WORKPLACE: PROPOSALS FOR A BETTER SYSTEM 77–100 (Earl Pollack & Deborah Keimig ed. 1987). All published estimates of occupational illnesses and diseases have been termed a "gross underestimate." Harvey Hilaski, *Understanding Statistics on Occupational Illnesses*, MONTHLY LABOR REVIEW, Mar. 1981, at 25. For an overview of the problems involved in identifying occupational diseases, see PETER BARTH & H. HUNT, WORKERS' COMPENSATION AND WORK-RELATED ILLNESSES AND DISEASES (1980); Rainer Müller, *A Patient in Need of Care: German Occupational Health Statistics*, in THE SOCIAL HISTORY OF OCCUPATIONAL HEALTH 127 (Paul Weindling ed. 1985); OECD, EMPLOYMENT OUTLOOK, July 1990, at 105–22.

7. William Krizan, Hazel Bradford, & Steven Setzer, *Law of Jungle is Gaining Strength*, ENR, Jan. 31, 1994, at 70; Jon Nordheimer, *Pressure of Costs Drives Some Contractors to Stress Work Safety*, N.Y. TIMES, Aug. 21, 1993, at 25, col. 1 (Lexis).

8. HERMAN SOMERS & ANNE SOMERS, WORKMEN'S COMPENSATION: PREVENTION, INSURANCE, AND REHABILITATION OF OCCUPATIONAL DISABILITY 6 (1954).

9. EDISON BOWERS, IS IT SAFE TO WORK? A STUDY OF INDUSTRIAL ACCIDENTS 1, 2 (1930).

10. E. DOWNEY, WORKMEN'S COMPENSATION 1 (1924).

11. E. DOWNEY, HISTORY OF WORK ACCIDENT INDEMNITY IN IOWA 2–3, 4, 5 (1912).

12. On the rhetoric of war and injury, see ELAINE SCARRY, THE BODY IN PAIN: THE MAKING AND UNMAKING OF THE WORLD 60–157 (1987 [1985]).

13. *See, e.g.*, 116 CONG. REC. 38,385 (1970) (Rep. Dent); *id.* at 38,387 (Rep. Gaydos).

14. *Occupational Safety and Health Act of 1969: Hearings Before the Select Subcomm. on Labor of the House Comm. on Education and Labor*, 91st Cong., 1st Sess. 112 (1969).

15. For an example of an author so intent on conceptualizing *accident* in terms of the "contract-form of employment" that he loses sight of its rootedness in a profit-driven economy, see Karl Figlio, *What Is an Accident?*, in THE SOCIAL HISTORY OF OCCUPATIONAL HEALTH at 180.

16. One such question, for example, is whether deaths occurring during travel to and from work should be included. In West Germany, for example, accidents on the way to and from work are compensable but are tabulated separately; in recent years, they have accounted for about one-third of industrial fatalities. BERICHT DER BUNDESREGIERUNG ÜBER DEN STAND DER UNFALLVERHÜTUNG UND DAS UNFALLGESCHEHEN IN DER BUNDESREPUBLIK DEUTSCHLAND: UNFALLVERHÜTUNGSBERICHT 1991, tab. 1 at 54, tab. 3 at 56 (Bundestag Doc. 12/3988, 1992). Under the "Going and Coming Rule," absent special circumstances such as employer-provided transportation, injuries sustained while traveling to and from work are not compensable under state workers' compensation statutes in the United States. 1 ARTHUR LARSON, THE LAW OF WORKMEN'S COMPENSATION, § 15.11 at 4–3 (1992). The claim that many state workers' compensation boards count commuting deaths as job-related is, without qualification, incorrect. *See* J. Leigh, *Estimates of the Probability of Job-Related Death in 347 Occupations*, 29 J. OCCUPATIONAL MED. 510 (1987). *See also* NIOSH, FATAL INJURIES TO WORKERS IN THE UNITED STATES, 1980–1989: A DECADE OF SURVEILLANCE: NATIONAL PROFILE, App. I (1993) (excluding such deaths); 1 INT'L LAB. OFFICE, ENCYCLOPAEDIA OF OCCUPATIONAL HEALTH AND SAFETY 12–13 (1972); OECD EMPLOYMENT OUTLOOK, July 1989, at 136 (varying practices in European countries).

17. *See* Larence Hanrahan & Michael Moll, *Injury Surveillance*, AM. J. PUB. HEALTH, Dec. 1989 (Supp.), at 38.

18. Early on researchers recognized that construction workers were also subject to severe occupational illness and disease risks; lead poisoning, for example, was a leading cause of death among painters. U.S. BLS, Bulletin 207: CAUSES OF DEATH BY OCCUPATION: OCCUPATIONAL MORTALITY EXPERIENCE OF THE METROPOLITAN LIFE INSURANCE CO. INDUSTRIAL DEPARTMENT, 1911–1913, at 50–52 (1917); U.S. DIVISION OF LABOR STANDARDS, Bulletin No. 7: RECENT CHANGES IN THE PAINTERS' TRADE (1936) (by Alice Hamilton). On such typical bricklayers' health problems as back injuries, see STUDENTERFRONTEN VED AARHUS UNIVERSITET, MURERRAPPORTEN 58–69 (n.d. [ca. 1972]).

19. Jimmie Hinze & Jair Roxo, *Is Injury Occurrence Related to Lunar Cycles?* 110 J. CONSTRUCTION ENGINEERING & MGMT. 409 (1984).

20. Gregg LaBar, *Breaking New Ground in Construction Safety*, OCCUPATIONAL HAZARDS, May 1992, at 58.

21. PATRICIA COHEN, A CALCULATING PEOPLE: THE SPREAD OF NUMERACY IN EARLY AMERICA 207 (1982).

22. C.H. Mark, *Our Murderous Industrialism*, 12 WORLD TO-DAY 97 (1907).

23. WERNER SOMBART, WARUM GIBT ES IN DEN VEREINIGTEN STAATEN KEINEN SOZIALISMUS? 126 (1906).

24. Werner Sombart, *Studien zur Entwicklungsgeschichte des nordamerikanischen Proletariats: I. Einleitung*, 21 ARCHIV FÜR SOZIALWISSENSCHAFT UND SOZIALPOLITIK 210, 212 (1905).

25. *See* U.S. BUREAU OF THE CENSUS, HISTORICAL STATISTICS OF THE UNITED STATES, COLONIAL TIMES TO 1970, pt. 1, ser. M 271 at 607 and pt. 2, ser. Q. 404 at 740 (bicentennial ed. 1975); 2 HARRY MILLIS & ROYAL MONTGOMERY, THE ECONOMICS OF LABOR: LABOR'S RISKS AND SOCIAL INSURANCE 187 (1938).

26. 13 ENCYCLOPAEDIA OF THE SOCIAL SCIENCES 504 (1937) (s.v. "Safety Movement").

27. U.S. BLS, Bull. No. 234: The Safety Movement in the Iron and Steel Industry 1907 to 1917, at 13 (1918) (written by Lucian Chaney & Hugh Hanna).

28. U.S. BLS, Bull. No. 157: Industrial Accident Statistics 101 (1915) (by Frederick Hoffman) (data for 1907–1912); Frederick Hoffman, *Industrial Accidents*, in U.S. Bureau of Labor, Bulletin, No. 78, Sept. 1908, at 417, 458 (data for 1897–1906).

29. Karl Marx, Zur Kritik der Politischen Ökonomie (Manuskript 1861–1863), in II:3.1 Karl Marx [and] Friedrich Engels, Gesamtausgabe (MEGA) 324 (1976) (written in English).

30. *See* Paul Uselding, *In Dispraise of the Muckrakers: United States Occupational Mortality, 1890–1910*, in 1 Research in Economic History 334 (Paul Uselding ed. 1976).

31. Arthur Reeves, *Our Industrial Juggernaut*, 16 Everybody's Mag. 147, 148 (1907).

32. Crystal Eastman, Work Accidents and the Law (1910).

33. Upton Sinclair, The Jungle (1906); Gabriel Kolko, The Triumph of Conservatism: A Reinterpretation of American History, 1900–1916, at 98–108 (1977 [1963]).

34. William Hard, *Making Steel and Killing Men*, 17 Everybody's Mag. 579, 581 (1907).

35. *The "Casualty List" of American Industries*, 96 Sci. Am. 126 (1907) (editorial).

36. Samuel Gompers, *Industrial Slaughter and the "Enlightened Employers,"* 14 Am. Federationist 548, 549 (1907).

37. Samuel Gompers, *The Price We Pay*, 17 Am. Federationist 665 (1910).

38. John Mitchell, *Burden of Industrial Accidents*, 38 Annals Am. Acad. Pol. & Soc. Sci. 76, 77, 78 (1911).

39. *See e.g.*, National Safe Workplace Institute, Failed Opportunities: The Decline of U.S. Job Safety in the 1980s 5–6 (1988); *idem*, Unmet Needs: Making American Work Safe for the 1990s, at 9–10 (1989); R. Blake Smith, *Getting to the Bottom of High Accident Rates*, Occupational Health & Safety, June 1993, at 34. For the underlying employment data, see U.S. BLS, Bull. 1865: Handbook of Labor Statistics—Reference Edition, tab. 39 & 46 at 105, 118 (1975); Employment and Earnings, Dec. 1993, tab. A-25 at 37. High construction accident rates relative to those in manufacturing appear to be invariant in capitalist, socialist, and underdeveloped countries although the levels in socialist countries were lower. *See e.g.*, International Labour Office, Year Book of Labour Statistics, 1974, at 724–28 (1974); *idem*, Year Book of Labour Statistics, 1992, at 997–1052 (1992).

40. Luke Grant, The National Erectors' Association and the International Association of Bridge and Structural Ironworkers 8 (1971 [1915]).

41. Frederick Klein, *Ironworker Tom West Wrestles Steel Beams High Above the Ground*, Wall St. J., Mar. 4, 1971, at 1, col. 1. The membership's annual fatality rate was still close to one per cent. For additional corroboration, see *Injury Rates in Construction Occupations, 1948*, 70 Monthly Lab. Rev. 387, 388 (1950).

42. *Reducing Casualties in Construction Work*, 72 Engineering News 145 (1914).

43. Ethelbert Stewart, *Accidents in the Construction Industry*, 28 Monthly Lab. Rev. 63, 65 (1929).

44. The British factory acts as early as 1844 required employers to equip machines with guards. An Act to amend the Laws relating to Labour in Factories, 7 & 8 Vict., c. 15, §§ 21, 59 (1844); An Act to consolidate and amend the Law relating to Factories and Workshops, 41 & 42 Vict., c. 16, § 5 (1878); An Act to consolidate with Amendment the Factories and Workshop Acts, 1 Edw. 7, c. 22, § 10 (1901). *See generally*, P. Bartrip & S. Burman, The Wounded Soldiers of Industry: Industrial Compensation Policy 1833–1897, at 54–96 (1983). The Industrial Code for the North German Confederation of 1869 obligated covered employers to provide and maintain all facilities necessary to protect their workers against dangers to life and health. Gewerbeordnung für den Norddeutschen Bund, 21 June 1869, BGBl des Norddeutschen Bundes, § 107 at 270. Despite the expansive scope of this provision, the state failed to enforce it vigorously. Lothar Machtan, *Workers' Insurance Versus Protection of the Workers: State Social Policy in Imperial Germany*, in The Social History of Occupational Health at 209. The 1891 amendments to the Industrial Code added the

weasel words, "as the nature of the operation permits." Gesetz, betreffend Abänderung der Gewerbeordnung, 1 June 1891, RGBl, § 120a at 5.

45. C. LEGIEN, AUS AMERIKAS ARBEITERBEWEGUNG 51, 52, 54 (1914). *See also* MARTIN WAGNER, AMERIKANISCHE BAUWIRTSCHAFT 27, 43 (1925).

46. 26 STATISTISCHES JAHRBUCH FÜR DAS DEUTSCHE REICH 1905, at 268 (1905) (with data for 1886 to 1903). This was the last year in which the Imperial Statistical Office printed the total of all fatalities since the inception of the Accident Prevention Law. For an analysis showing that the German law placed the state's imprimatur on the principle that industrial work entailed an unavoidable risk for workers and transformed the principle of prevention-oriented liability into a purely (and non-fully) compensatory compulsory insurance scheme, see Lothar Machtan, *Risikoversicherung statt Gesundheitsschutz für Arbeiter: Zur Entstehung der Unfallversicherungsgesetzgebung im Bismarck-Reich*, 13 LEVIATHAN 420 (1985).

47. 1 KARL MARX, DAS KAPITAL: KRITIK DER POLITISCHEN ÖKONOMIE 253 (1867 & photo reprint 1959).

48. *See* DAVID GORDON, RICHARD EDWARDS, & MICHAEL REICH, SEGMENTED WORK, DIVIDED WORKERS: THE HISTORICAL TRANSFORMATION OF LABOR IN THE UNITED STATES 127–62 (1982).

49. Lorenzo Lewelling ["The Tramp Circular"], DAILY CAPITAL [Topeka], Dec. 5, 1893, reprinted in THE POPULIST MIND 330, 331 (Norman Pollack ed. 1967) (populist governor of Kansas).

50. ISAAC HOURWICH, IMMIGRATION AND LABOR: THE ECONOMIC ASPECTS OF EUROPEAN IMMIGRATION TO THE UNITED STATES 486 (1912).

51. SIXTEENTH ANNUAL REPORT OF THE COMMISSIONER OF LABOR, 1901: STRIKES AND LOCK-OUTS 469–74, 478–83 (1901).

52. For a sustained argument that class struggle took the form of individual litigation, see Anthony Bale, Compensation Crisis: The Value and Meaning of Work-Related Injuries and Illnesses in the United States, 1842–1932 (Ph.D. diss., Brandeis University 1986).

53. MARX, ZUR KRITIK DER POLITISCHEN ÖKONOMIE (MANUSKRIPT 1861–1863) at 162

54. WILLIAM GRAEBNER, COAL-MINING SAFETY IN THE PROGRESSIVE PERIOD: THE POLITICAL ECONOMY OF REFORM 127–39 (1976).

55. BARTRIP & BURMAN, THE WOUNDED SOLDIERS OF INDUSTRY at 37–53 (on nineteenth-century data collection by factory inspectors); SAFETY AND HEALTH AT WORK: REPORT OF THE COMMITTEE 1970–72, at 134–38, 161 (Cmnd. 5034, 1972); SANDRA DAWSON, PAUL WILLMAN, ALAN CLINTON, & MARTIN BAMFORD, SAFETY AT WORK: THE LIMITS OF SELF-REGULATION 27 (1988).

56. [U.K.] DEPARTMENT OF EMPLOYMENT AND PRODUCTIVITY, BRITISH LABOUR STATISTICS: HISTORICAL ABSTRACT 1886–1968, tab. 200 at 399–400 (1971); [U.K.] CENTRAL STATISTICAL OFFICE, ANNUAL ABSTRACT OF STATISTICS 1974, No. 111, tab. 65 at 75 (1974); *idem*, ANNUAL ABSTRACT OF STATISTICS 1984, No. 120, tab. 3.36 at 71 (1984); *idem*, ANNUAL ABSTRACT OF STATISTICS 1992, No. 128, tab. 3.35 at 72 (1992); *idem*, ANNUAL ABSTRACT OF STATISTICS 1993, No. 129, tab. 3.35 at 70 (1993).

57. *Legislative Hearings on H.R. 1063, the Construction Safety, Health, and Education Improvement Act of 1991: Hearings Before the Subcomm. on Health and Safety of the House Comm. on Education and Labor*, 102d Cong., 1st Sess. 257 (Serial No. 102–15, 1991) (testimony of Dr. Knut Ringen); THOMAS McGARITY & SIDNEY SHAPIRO, WORKERS AT RISK: THE FAILED PROMISE OF THE OCCUPATIONAL SAFETY AND HEALTH ADMINISTRATION 4–5 (1993). Since the ILO data on fatality rates that Ringen used are based on at four different national bases (per man-hours, man-years, workers exposed to risk, and persons employed), it is unclear how Ringen reduced them all to a per 1,000 workers common basis. *See* ILO, YEAR BOOK OF LABOUR STATISTICS 1992 at 1042; INTERNATIONAL LABOUR OFFICE, CURRENT INTERNATIONAL RECOMMENDATIONS ON LABOUR STATISTICS 1988 EDITION 101–104 (1988).

58. Reeve, *Our Industrial Juggernaut* at 147.

59. JOHN COMMONS & JOHN ANDREWS, PRINCIPLES OF LABOR LEGISLATION 160–63 (4th ed. 1967 [1916]).

60. Hoffman, *Industrial Accidents* at 421. *See generally,* [NEW YORK STATE COMMISSION ON EMPLOYERS LIABILITY], REPORT TO THE STATE OF NEW YORK: FIRST REPORT 191–93, 197 (1910); I. RUBINOW, SOCIAL INSURANCE: WITH SPECIAL REFERENCE TO AMERICAN CONDITIONS 49–85 (1913).

61. Act of Mar, 3, 1901, ch. 866, 31 Stat. 1446; Act of May 6, 1910, ch. 208, 36 Stat. 350.

62. U.S. BLS, Bull. No. 157: INDUSTRIAL ACCIDENT STATISTICS at 7.

63. Reeve, *Our Industrial Juggernaut* at 156.

64. Hoffman, *Industrial Accidents* at 417–18.

65. U.S. BLS, Bulletin No. 157: INDUSTRIAL ACCIDENT STATISTICS.

66. 1 U.S. COMMISSION ON INDUSTRIAL RELATIONS, INDUSTRIAL RELATIONS: FINAL REPORT AND TESTIMONY, S. DOC. No. 415, 64th Cong., 1st Sess. 70 (1916).

67. Royal Meeker, *The Why and How of Uniform Industrial Accident Statistics for the United States,* in U.S. BLS, Bulletin 210: PROCEEDINGS OF THE THIRD ANNUAL MEETING OF THE INTERNATIONAL ASSOCIATION OF INDUSTRIAL ACCIDENT BOARDS AND COMMISSIONS 91 (1917 [1916]).

68. Ethelbert Stewart, *Are Accidents Increasing?* 23 MONTHLY LAB. REV. 46 (1926); *idem, Industrial Accidents in the United States,* ANNALS, Jan. 1926, at 1. *See also* Leonard Hatch, *The Problem of National Accident Statistics,* 23 MONTHLY LAB. REV. 722 (1926).

69. *See* U.S. BLS, Bull. No. 203: WORKMEN'S COMPENSATION LAWS OF THE UNITED STATES AND FOREIGN COUNTRIES (1917).

70. Unfallversicherungsgesetz, July 6, 1884, RGBl 69. Coverage was broad, and employers were required to report deaths to the police; *id.* §§ 1, 51–52 at 69, 91. On the origins of social insurance as an attempt to control the working class, see GASTON RIMLINGER, WELFARE POLICY AND INDUSTRIALIZATION IN EUROPE, AMERICA, AND RUSSIA 112–22 (1971); HANS-ULRICH WEHLER, BISMARCK UND DER IMPERIALISMUS 459–64 (1976 [1969]); Machtan, *Workers' Insurance.*

71. *See* 7 HANDWÖRTERBUCH DER STAATSWISSENSCHAFTEN 260, 285 (J. Conrad et al. 2d ed. 1901) (s.v. "Unfallstatistik" and "Unfallversicherung"). Even the German system was not universal. *See* 26 STATISTISCHES JAHRBUCH FÜR DAS DEUTSCHE REICH 1905, at 268 n.1 (1905); Müller, *A Patient in Need of Care.*

72. Margaret Gadsby, *Inadequacy of Industrial Accident Statistics Published in State Reports,* 12 MONTHLY LAB. REV. 167 (1921). *See also* U.S. BLS, Bull. No. 339: STATISTICS OF INDUSTRIAL ACCIDENTS IN THE UNITED STATES 1–8 (1923) (by Lucian Chaney).

73. 81 ENGINEERING NEWS-RECORD 298 (1918).

74. W. STARRETT, SKYSCRAPERS AND THE MEN WHO BUILD THEM 301 (1928).

75. Carl Hookstadt, *Estimated Annual Number and Cost of Industrial Accidents in the United States,* 17 MONTHLY LAB. REV. 991, tab. 4 at 996 (1923). These figures included all gainfully employed persons; among employees, fatalities totaled 21,232.

76. U.S. DEPARTMENT OF LABOR, ELEVENTH ANNUAL REPORT OF THE SECRETARY OF LABOR FOR THE FISCAL YEAR ENDED JUNE 30, 1923, at 59 (1923). *See also* Charles Verrill, *Industrial Accident and Compensation Statistics,* 12 AM. ECON. REV. 137 (Mar. 1922) (Supp.).

77. JOSEPH DUNCAN & WILLIAM SHELTON, REVOLUTION IN UNITED STATES GOVERNMENT STATISTICS: 1926–1976, at 18 (U.S. Dept. of Commerce, 1978); LAURENCE SCHMECKEBIER, THE STATISTICAL WORK OF THE NATIONAL GOVERNMENT 132–37 (1925).

78. For a typology of arguments in favor of government data collecting, see Steven Kelman, *The Political Foundations of American Statistical Policy,* in THE POLITICS OF NUMBERS 275, 280 (William Alonso & Paul Starr ed. 1987).

79. *Division of Safety: Hearings Before the House Committee on Labor,* 69th Cong., 1st Sess. 1 (1926) (H.R. 11886).

80. *Id.* at 3 (Rep. Rathbone).

81. *To Create a Division of Safety in the Department of Labor: Hearing Before the Senate Committee on Education and Labor,* 69th Cong., 1st Sess. 39 (1926).

82. *Id.* at 39, 45.

83. *See, e.g.*, ROBERT SMITH, THE OCCUPATIONAL SAFETY AND HEALTH ACT: ITS GOALS AND ITS ACHIEVEMENTS (1976).

84. 68 CONG. REC. 5030 (1927); *see also id.* at 1015–18; S. REP. No. 1288, 69th Cong., 2d Sess. (1927).

85. William Wheeler, *Results Through Voluntary Cooperation in Accident Prevention in Construction*, in 1929 TRANSACTIONS OF THE NATIONAL SAFETY COUNCIL: EIGHTEENTH ANNUAL SAFETY CONGRESS 1:650, 655 (1929) (executive secretary of the Committee on Accident Prevention of the Building Trades Employers' Association of the City of New York).

86. Henry Mock, *Penalty the American Nation Pays for Speed*, 25 MONTHLY LAB. REV. 55 (1927).

87. U.S. BLS, Bull. No. 425: RECORD OF INDUSTRIAL ACCIDENTS IN THE UNITED STATES TO 1925, at 104 (1927).

88. NATIONAL CONFERENCE ON CONSTRUCTION, REPORTS: GENERAL MEETING, pt. 13 at 3 (1932).

89. U.S. BLS, Bull. No. 490: STATISTICS OF INDUSTRIAL ACCIDENTS IN THE UNITED STATES TO THE END OF 1927, at 1–10 (1929).

90. *Industrial Injuries in the United States, 1917 to 1932*, 38 MONTHLY LAB. REV. 1093, 1094 (1934).

91. Max Kossoris & Swen Kjaer, *Industrial Injuries in the United States During 1936*, 47 MONTHLY LAB. REV. 18 (1938).

92. U.S. BLS, Bull. 667: MANUAL ON INDUSTRIAL INJURY STATISTICS 1 (1940).

93. On the NSC's ambivalence toward the slogan, see Dianne Bennett & William Graebner, *Safety First: Slogan and Symbol of the Industrial Safety Movement*, 68 J. ILL. STATE HIST. SOC'Y 243, 255–56 (1975).

94. U.S. BLS, Bull. No. 304: PROCEEDINGS OF THE EIGHTH ANNUAL MEETING OF THE INTERNATIONAL ASSOCIATION OF INDUSTRIAL ACCIDENT BOARDS AND COMMISSIONS 63 (1922 [1921]) (discussion contribution by A. J. Pillsbury, Comm'r, Cal. Indus. Accident Comm'n).

95. *See, e.g.*, U.S. BUREAU OF THE CENSUS, STATISTICAL ABSTRACT OF THE UNITED STATES: 1992, tab. 665 at 419 (112th ed. 1992) (using NSC estimates). When the Census Bureau began publishing the BLS injury rates, it classified them among "labor force" data. *Idem*, STATISTICAL ABSTRACT OF THE UNITED STATES: 1944–45, tab. 172 at 171 (1945).

96. *See, e.g.*, MINISTÈRE DU TRAVAIL, ANNUAIRE STATISTIQUE—1922, at 149 (1923); CENTRAL STATISTICAL OFFICE, ANNUAL ABSTRACT OF STATISTICS 1992, tab. 3.35 at 72; STATISTISCHES BUNDESAMT, STATISTISCHES JAHRBUCH 1976 FÜR DIE BUNDESREPUBLIK DEUTSCHLAND, tab. 21.3.2 at 389 (1976); STATISTISK CENTRALBYRÅ, STATISTISK ÅRBOK 1991, tab. 136 at 116 (1991); STATISTISKA CENTRALBYRÅN, STATISTISK ÅRBOK FÖR SVERIGE 1991, tab. 370 at 323 (1991); BUNDESAMT FÜR STATISTIK, STATISTISCHES JAHRBUCH DER SCHWEIZ 1991, tab. 13.9 at 262 (1990).

97. Act of Aug. 13, 1953, Pub. L. No. 259, 67 Stat. 569. This federal charter does not affect the NSC's nongovernmental status.

98. *See* Don Lescohier, *Working Conditions*, in 3 HISTORY OF LABOR IN THE UNITED STATES, 1896–1932, at 1, 366–70 (1935); DAVID BRODY, STEELWORKERS IN AMERICA: THE NONUNION ERA 164–68 (1969 [1960]); Lawrence Friedman & Jack Ladinsky, *Social Change and the Law of Industrial Accidents*, 67 COLUM. L. REV. 50 (1967); JAMES WEINSTEIN, THE CORPORATE IDEAL IN THE LIBERAL STATE: 1900–1918, at 40–61 (1968); DAVID NOBLE, AMERICA BY DESIGN: SCIENCE, TECHNOLOGY, AND THE RISE OF CORPORATE CAPITALISM 289–92 (1979 [1977]).

99. CHARLES NOBLE, LIBERALISM AT WORK: THE RISE AND FALL OF OSHA 43–45 (1986). *See also* JOSEPH PAGE & MARY-WIN O'BRIEN, BITTER WAGES: RALPH NADER'S STUDY GROUP REPORT ON DISEASE AND INJURY ON THE JOB 149–65 (1973); DANIEL BERMAN, DEATH ON THE JOB: OCCUPATIONAL HEALTH AND SAFETY STRUGGLES IN THE UNITED STATES 74–81 (1978).

100. NSC, ACCIDENT FACTS 1993 EDITION at 112.

101. NSC, "Documentation of National Safety Council Statistics Department Estimating Procedures for Motor-Vehicle, Work, Home, and Public Deaths and Death Rates" 2, 7–8 (Feb. 1982).

102. NSC, "Documentation" at 8, Appendix 8.

103. U.S. CONGRESS, OFFICE OF TECHNOLOGY ASSESSMENT, PREVENTING ILLNESS AND INJURY IN THE WORKPLACE 31 (1985).

104. NSC, ACCIDENT FACTS 1993 EDITION at 112–13; [Stephanie Brand & Alan Hoskin], "Allocation Factor Investigation' (n.d. [1993]). *See also* U.S. OCCUPATIONAL SAFETY & HEALTH ADMIN., ANALYSIS OF CONSTRUCTION FATALITIES—THE OSHA DATA BASE 1985–1989, at 75 (1990) ("Although the same equations are still used, the original data giving the rationale is no longer available").

105. *Occupational Safety and Health Act Review, 1974: Hearings Before the Subcomm. on Labor of the Senate Comm. on Labor and Public Welfare*, 93d Cong., 2d Sess. 92–93 (1974).

106. The NSC submitted a written supplement to its testimony to the committee, which merely stated that whereas the NSC "precisely tabulated" motor-vehicle deaths, it did not do so with regard to work, home, or public fatalities; it failed to explain its method for "estimating what the counts should be." *Occupational Safety and Health Act Review, 1974* at 909, 910.

107. NSC, "Documentation" at 8

108. Telephone interview with Alan Hoskin, NSC, Itasca, IL (Feb. 11, 1994, 11:00 a.m.). BERMAN, DEATH ON THE JOB at 39, inverts the absurdity of the procedure by charging that the absolute figures "were given a spurious appearance of accuracy by the inclusion of annual percentage changes."

109. NSC, "Documentation" at 1.

110. Untitled and undated information sheet distributed by the NSC.

111. JEROME GORDON, ALLAN AKMAN, & MICHAEL BROOKS, INDUSTRIAL SAFETY STATISTICS: A RE-EXAMINATION 189–90 (1971).

112. *Occupational Safety and Health Act, 1970: Hearings Before the Subcomm. on Labor of the Senate Comm. on Labor and Public Welfare*, pt. 2, 91st Cong., 1st & 2d Sess. 1113 (1970).

113. NICHOLAS ASHFORD, CRISIS IN THE WORKPLACE: OCCUPATIONAL DISEASE AND INJURY 46 (1976). For alternative injury rate statistics showing a stable or declining trend in the pre-OSHA period, see W. VISCUSI, RISK BY CHOICE: REGULATING HEALTH AND SAFETY IN THE WORKPLACE 28–31 (1983).

114. NSC, ACCIDENT FACTS 1973 EDITION 28 (1973).

115. For a (not very persuasive) explanation of a similar statistically inaccurate statement against interest—namely, Census Bureau data showing stagnation in real family income during the 1970s—see Christopher Jencks, *The Politics of Income Measurement*, in THE POLITICS OF NUMBERS 83, 126–31 (William Alonso & Paul Starr ed. 1987).

116. *Occupational Health and Safety Act, 1970: Hearings Before the Subcomm. on Labor of the Senate Comm. on Labor and Public Welfare*, Pt. 1 at 630.

117. U.S. BLS, Bulletin No. 276: STANDARDIZATION OF INDUSTRIAL ACCIDENT STATISTICS 73 (1920).

118. Max Kossoris & Swen Kjaer, *Industrial Injuries in the United States During 1936*, 47 MONTHLY LAB. REV. 18, 20, 23, 26 (1938).

119. Max Kossoris & Swen Kjaer, *Industrial Accidents in the United States During 1937*, 48 MONTHLY LAB. REV. 597, 599 (1939).

120. Max Kossoris & Swen Kjaer, *Industrial Injuries in the United States During 1939*, 51 MONTHLY LAB. REV. 86, 89 (1940).

121. U.S. BLS, Bulletin No. 1004: WORK INJURIES IN CONSTRUCTION, 1948–49, at 2–3 (1950).

122. U.S. BLS, Bull. No. 1016: HANDBOOK OF LABOR STATISTICS 1950 EDITION 175 (1951).

123. U.S. BLS, Bull. No. 1458: HANDBOOK OF METHODS FOR SURVEYS AND STUDIES 205 (1966).

124. *See, e.g.,* U.S. BLS, Bull. No. 916: HANDBOOK OF LABOR STATISTICS, 1947 EDITION, tab. G-2 at 164 (1948); NSC, ACCIDENT FACTS 1973 EDITION at 29; *supra* tab. 1. Neither the BLS nor NSC explained why their fatality figures diverged for several years.

125. U.S. BLS, Bull. No. 1025: WORK INJURIES IN THE UNITED STATES DURING 1949, at 1 n.3 (1951).

126. U.S. Bureau of Labor Standards, Bull. 175: THE PRESIDENT'S CONFERENCE ON OCCUPATIONAL SAFETY: PROCEEDINGS MAY 4–6, 1954, at 7–8 (1954) (Ewan Clague).

127. U.S. BLS, HANDBOOK OF METHODS FOR SURVEYS AND STUDIES at 205.

128. *Id.* at 205, 206. From several statements it is possible to surmise that the fatality figures were not enumerations at all but merely derived from some observed patterns of deaths as a share of all injuries. Thus the BLS spoke in several places of the data as "the percent of disabling injuries resulting in death, permanent impairment, and temporary-total disability." *Id.* at 197; *see also id.* at 198, 204.

129. UNITED STATES OF AMERICA STANDARDS INSTITUTE, USA STANDARD METHOD OF RECORDING AND MEASURING WORK INJURY EXPERIENCE 8 (1967), *reprinted in Occupational Safety and Health Act, 1970: Hearings Before the Subcomm. on Labor of the Senate Comm. on Labor and Public Welfare,* pt. 2 at 1181; COUNTING INJURIES AND ILLNESSES IN THE WORKPLACE at 12–13; Lyle Schauer & Thomas Ryder, *New Approach to Occupational Safety and Health Statistics,* MONTHLY LAB. REV., Mar. 1972, at 14.

130. *Occupational Health and Safety Act, 1970: Hearings Before the Subcomm. on Labor of the Senate Comm. on Labor and Public Welfare,* pt. 1 at 628.

131. U.S. BLS, Bull. 1798: OCCUPATIONAL INJURIES AND ILLNESSES BY INDUSTRY: JULY 1-DECEMBER 31, 1971, at 25, 31 (1973); NSC, ACCIDENTS FACTS 1973 EDITION at 33.

132. *Construction Safety, Health and Education Improvement Act of 1989: Hearing Before the Senate Comm. on Labor and Human Resources,* 101st Cong., 1st Sess. 106 (1989) (testimony of Barry Cole, manager, construction safety consulting firm). This ignorance did not prevent Senator Dodd from calculating at the same hearing that "every 2 hours, three construction workers" are killed. *Id.* at 2.

133. 3 KARL MARX, DAS KAPITAL: KRITIK DER POLITISCHEN ÖKONOMIE, in 25 KARL MARX [&] FRIEDRICH ENGELS, WERKE 99 (1964 [1894]) (describing British factory inspectors' reports).

134. *See, e.g.,* THE PRESIDENT'S REPORT ON OCCUPATIONAL SAFETY AND HEALTH 1975, tab. 14 at 108 (1979). The statutory authority is at 29 U.S.C. § 675 (1988).

135. 29 C.F.R. § 1904.12(c) (1993).

136. 29 C.F.R. § 1904.2(a) (1993); Paul Seligman et al., *Compliance with OSHA Recordkeeping Requirements,* 78 AM. J. PUB. HEALTH 1218 (1988); U.S. GAO, OCCUPATIONAL SAFETY & HEALTH: ASSURING ACCURACY IN EMPLOYER INJURY AND ILLNESS RECORDS 3 (1988).

137. U.S. BLS, Bull. 2399: OCCUPATIONAL INJURIES AND ILLNESSES IN THE UNITED STATES BY INDUSTRY, 1990, at 1 (1992) (italics added).

138. Eileen McNeely, *Who's Counting Anyway? The Problem with Occupational Safety and Health Statistics,* 33 J. OCCUPATIONAL MED. 1071 (1991).

139. Anthony Suruda & Edward Emmett, *Counting Recognized Occupational Deaths in the United States,* 30 J. OCCUPATIONAL MED. 868 (1988).

140. *See* 2 WOLFGANG DÄUBLER, DAS ARBEITSRECHT: EIN LEITFADEN FÜR ARBEITNEHMER 127 (1979). Even in proposing release of firm-level data to the public, the U.S. Department of Labor worried that groups might "'harass' individual employers." DAILY LAB. REP., May 11, 1994 (Lexis).

141. While continuing to acknowledge BLS's need for confidentiality, the OSHAdm has proposed moving in the direction of requiring larger employers to submit the logs to the OSHAdm. U.S. GAO, OCCUPATIONAL SAFETY AND HEALTH: CHANGES NEEDED IN THE COMBINED FEDERAL-STATE APPROACH 36, 69 (1994); DAILY LAB. REP., Mar, 23, 1994; *id.,* May 2, 1994 (Lexis).

142. 29 U.S.C. § 657(c)(1) (1988); 29 C.F.R. § 1904.7(a) (1993).

143. FED. R. CIV. P. 11.

144. *See, e.g.*, Dole v. Trinity Industries, 904 F.2d 867 (3d Cir. 1990).

145. *OSHA Enforcement Policy: Hearings Before a Subcomm. of the House Comm. on Government Operations*, 98th Cong., 1st Sess. 13 (1983) (statement of Thorne Auchter, ass't sec'y of labor for OSH); COUNTING INJURIES AND ILLNESSES IN THE WORKPLACE at 47–48, 111–12; LAWRENCE WHITE, HUMAN DEBRIS: THE INJURED WORKER IN AMERICA 153 (1982).

146. RAYMOND LEVITT & NANCY SAMELSON, CONSTRUCTION SAFETY MANAGEMENT 152 (1987).

147. ASSOCIATED GENERAL CONTRACTORS OF AMERICA, INC., MANUAL OF ACCIDENT PREVENTION IN CONSTRUCTION x (3d ed. 1949 [1927]).

148. *But see* 1 INT'L LAB. OFFICE, ENCYCLOPAEDIA OF OCCUPATIONAL HEALTH AND SAFETY at 14 (discussing such a requirement).

149. 29 C.F.R. § 1904.8 (1993).

150. Clifford May, *Record Fines Are Imposed in Building Collapse That Killed*, N.Y. TIMES, Oct. 23, 1987, B1, at col. 2 (Lexis).

151. *Legislative Hearings on the Construction Safety, Health, and Education Improvement Act of 1990: Hearings Before the Subcomm. on Health and Safety of the House Comm. on Education and Labor*, 101st Cong., 2d Sess. 10–11 (1990) (Rep. Shays).

152. This figure includes illness fatalities for which the BLS published separate totals for the years 1971 to 1973.

153. Diane Cotter & Janet Macon, *Death in Industry, 1985: BLS Survey Findings*, MONTHLY LAB. REV., Apr. 1987, at 45, 47.

154. U.S. BLS, Bull. 2047: OCCUPATIONAL INJURIES AND ILLNESSES IN THE UNITED STATES BY INDUSTRY, 1977, at 5 (1980). For descriptions of the scope of the surveys earlier in the 1970s, see U.S. BLS, Rep. 438: OCCUPATIONAL SAFETY AND HEALTH STATISTICS: CONCEPTS AND METHODS (1975); U.S. BLS, Rep. 518: OCCUPATIONAL SAFETY AND HEALTH STATISTICS: CONCEPTS AND METHODS (1978).

155. The rates were 1.97 and 0.004 per 1,000 workers respectively. Barbara Marsh, *Chances of Getting Hurt Is Generally Far Higher at Smaller Companies*, WALL ST. J., Feb. 3, 1994, at A1, col. 1. According to OSHA data, 45 percent of all construction fatalities occur in workplaces with 25 or fewer employees. S. REP. NO. 558: CONSTRUCTION SAFETY, HEALTH, AND EDUCATION IMPROVEMENT ACT, 101st Cong., 2d Sess. 6 (1990).

156. An intermediate figure comes from a labor group estimation that three to four construction workers are killed daily. WALL ST. J., Feb. 22, 1994, A1, at 5.

157. COUNTING INJURIES AND ILLNESSES IN THE WORKPLACE at 56–60, 145, 148–49.

158. 29 U.S.C. §§ 652(6), 654 (1988).

159. Norman Root & David McCaffrey, *Providing More Information on Work Injury and Illness*, MONTHLY LAB. REV., Apr. 1978, at 18–19, 21 n.2 (citing 1976 Stanford Research Institute report).

160. 29 C.F.R. § 1904.8 (1993).

161. U.S. OSHA, ANALYSIS OF CONSTRUCTION FATALITIES at 3. The BLS data reported by OSHA are for some years identical with but for other years differ from those furnished by BLS itself. *Id.* at 53, 56.

162. *Id.* at 51–55.

163. Nancy Stout & Catherine Bell, *Effectiveness of Source Documents for Identifying Fatal Occupational Injuries: A Synthesis of Studies*, 81 AM. J. PUB. HEALTH 725 (1991).

164. Julie Russell & Carol Conroy, *Representativeness of Deaths Identified Through the Injury-at-Work Item on the Death Certificate: Implications for Surveillance*, 81 AM. J. PUB. HEALTH 1613 (1991).

165. Suzanne Kisner & David Fosbroke, *Injury Hazards in the Construction Industry*, 36 J. OCCUPATIONAL MED., Feb. 1994, at 137.

166. Nancy Stout-Wiegand, *Fatal Occupational Injuries in US Industries, 1984: Comparison of Two National Surveillance Systems*, 78 AM. J. PUB. HEALTH 1215 (1988).

167. Suruda & Emmett, *Counting Recognized Occupational Deaths in the United States* at 870.

168. Guy Toscano & Janice Windau, *Further Test of a Census Approach to Compiling Data on Fatal Work Injuries*, MONTHLY LAB. REV., Oct. 1991, at 114.

169. Susan Baker et al., *Fatal Occupational Injuries*, 248 J. AM. MED. ASS'N 692 (1982).

170. U.S. GAO, OCCUPATIONAL SAFETY AND HEALTH: ASSURING ACCURACY IN EMPLOYER INJURY AND ILLNESS RECORDS (HRD-89-23, 1988).

171. COUNTING INJURIES AND ILLNESSES IN THE WORKPLACE at 6. *See also* "News Conference with Robert Reich, Secretary of Labor, and William Barron, Acting Commissioner of the Bureau of Labor Statistics," Fed. News Serv., Oct. 1, 1993 (Lexis) (statement by Barron).

172. *See e.g.*, Arthur Oleinick et al., *Current Method of Estimating Severity for Occupational Injuries and Illnesses: Data from the 1986 Michigan Comprehensive Compensable Injury and Illness Database*, 23 AM. J. INDUS. MED. 231 (1993); Arthur Rubens, *Workplace Statistics Can't Cut to the Heart*, OCCUPATIONAL HEALTH AND SAFETY, Aug. 1993, at 64.

173. Guy Toscano, *The BLS Census of Fatal Occupational Injuries*, COMPENSATION & WORKING CONDITIONS, June 1991, at 1; Guy Toscano & Janice Windau, *Fatal Work Injuries: Results from the 1992 National Census*, MONTHLY LAB. REV., Oct. 1993, at 39, tab. 6 at 45; Tracy Jack & Mark Zak, *Results from the First National Census of Fatal Occupational Injuries, 1992*, COMPENSATION AND WORKING CONDITIONS, Dec. 1993, at 1; Janice Windau & Guy Toscano, *Workplace Homicides in 1992*, COMPENSATION & WORKING CONDITIONS, Feb. 1994, at 1, tab. 1 at 3; NSC, ACCIDENT FACTS 1993 EDITION at 27. The BLS later identified an additional 134 fatalities for 1992, raising the total to 6,217. The total for 1993 is 6,271. U.S. BLS, "National Census of Fatal Occupational Injuries, 1993" (News Release 94-384, Aug. 10, 1994).

174. Telephone interview with Alan Hoskin, manager, Statistics Dept., NSC, Mar. 23, 1994; telephone interview with Guy Toscano, Office of Safety, Health, and Working Conditions, BLS, Mar. 23, 1994; NSC, ACCIDENT FACTS 1993 EDITION at 39. See also Letitia Davis et al., *Data Sources for Fatality Surveillance in Commercial Fishing: Massachusetts, 1987–91*, in U.S. BLS, Rep. 870: FATAL WORKPLACE INJURIES IN 1992: A COLLECTION OF DATA AND ANALYSIS 42 (1994).

175. *See, e.g.*, Daniel Forbes, *The Growing Ranks of Contract Workers*, DUN'S BUSINESS MONTH, Mar. 1986, at 56; Louis Uchitelle, *Newest Corporate Refugees: Self-Employed But Low-Paid*, N.Y. Times, Nov. 15, 1993, at A1, col. 5 (nat. ed.); Marc Linder & Larry Zacharias, *Opening Coase's Other Black Box: Why Workers Submit to Vertical Integration into Firms*, 18 J. CORP. L. 371 (1993); *Spread of Illegal Home Sewing Is Fueled by Immigrants*, WALL ST. J., Mar. 15, 1994, at B1, col. 3; Robert Pear, *Clinton Health Care Plan Poses Question, 'Who Is an Employee?'*, N.Y. TIMES, Apr. 4, 1994, A1, at col. 4 (nat. ed.).

176. A half-century ago Congress considered a comprehensive "Workers' Social Insurance Act," which would not only have included self-employeds, but even conferred guaranteed annual incomes on them. *Social Insurance: Hearings Before the Senate Committee on Education and Labor*, 74th Cong., 2d Sess. 1–12 (1936). For an excellent overview of arguments in favor of equalization of treatment of self-employeds and employees in social insurance programs based on the former's equally insecure position as sellers of their labor power, see Olaf Sund, *Die Sozialpolitik für Selbständige*, in SOZIALPOLITIK UND SOZIALREFORM: EIN EINFÜHRENDES LEHR-UND HANDBUCH DER SOZIALPOLITIK 167 (Erik Boettcher ed. 1957).

177. *Legislative Hearings on the Construction Safety, Health, and Education Improvement Act of 1990* at 35 (testimony of Robert Georgine, president, Building & Construction Trades Dept., AFL-CIO). *See also* SAFETY AND HEALTH AT WORK: REPORT OF THE COMMITTEE 1970–72, at 55 ("There may . . . be situations where groups of self-employed persons may be to all intents and purposes in the same position as employees as regards their methods and conditions of work, that is to say their methods of work and working environment may not be within their direct control").

178. Guy Toscano & Janice Windau, *Fatal Work Injuries: Results from the 1992 National Census*, MONTHLY LAB. REV., Oct. 1992, at 39, tab. 2 at 41.

179. Catherine Bell, *Female Homicides in United States Workplaces, 1980–1985*, 81 AM. J. PUB. HEALTH 729 (1991); Jess Kraus, *Homicide While at Work: Persons, Industries, and Occupations at High Risk*, 77 AM. J. PUB. HEALTH 1285 (1987); Harold Davis, *Workplace Homicides of Texas Males*, 77 AM. J. PUB. HEALTH 1290 (1987).

180. Norman Root & Judy Daley, *Are Women Safer Workers? A New Look at the Data*, MONTHLY LAB. REV., Mar. 1981, at 3.

181. Hoffman, *Industrial Accidents* at 421 (U.K. data for 1895–1906); U.S. BLS, Bull. No. 157: INDUSTRIAL ACCIDENT STATISTICS, tab. 1 at 6 (U.S. data).

182. Windau & Toscano, *Workplace Homicides in 1992;* Guy Toscano, "1992 Census of Fatal Occupational Injuries: Safer and Healthier American Workplaces Through Improving Knowledge" (Presentation at Occupational Safety and Health State Plan Association Meeting, Washington, D.C., Jan. 30-Feb. 2, 1994). Female homicide victims in technical, sales, and administrative support occupations—which were the principal locus of workplace murders—accounted for one-half of all female homicides and more than one-quarter of all homicides in those occupations. Unpublished data furnished by U.S. BLS (Mar. 17, 1994); Windau & Toscano, *Workplace Homicides in 1992*, tab. 3 at 5. Despite the high proportion of homicides among female fatalities, women's work-related homicide rate is much lower than men's. E. Jenkins, *Occupational Injury Deaths Among Females: The US Experience for the Decade 1980 to 1989*, 4 ANNALS OF EPIDEMIOLOGY 146, 150 (1994).

183. NIOSH, FATAL INJURIES TO WORKERS IN THE UNITED STATES, 1980–1989, at 4. *See also* Catherine Bell, *Fatal Occupational Injuries in the United States, 1980 Through 1985*, 262 JAMA 3047 (1990).

184. Florence Kelley, *Our Lack of Statistics*, 38 ANNALS AM. ACAD. POL. & SOC. SCI. 94, 97 (1911).

185. "Dangerous weapons and dangerous people are offered greater Constitutional protection than most hazards in our environment." *Murder at Work*, 77 AM. J. PUB. HEALTH 1273 (1987) (editorial).

186. Dawn Castillo & E. Jenkins, *Industries and Occupations at High Risk for Work-Related Homicide*, 36 J. OCCUPATIONAL MED. 125 (1994); Windau & Toscano, *Workplace Homicides in 1992*, tab. 8 at 8. Some workplace homicides, especially those by subordinates against supervisors, may be (dangerous) employment-related. Thus a workers' compensation referee ruled that a black automobile worker's preexisting but nondisabling tendency toward paranoia had been "aggravated by his being unfairly assigned undesirable work in front of a hot oven, cheated out of advancement opportunities, addressed by a foreman as 'nigger' and 'boy,' denied medical benefits, . . . and, finally, fired after refusing to do a job he considered dangerous." *Michigan Rules Chrysler Must Pay Benefits to Man Who Killed* 3, WALL ST. J., Mar. 7, 1973, at 22, col. 3.

187. *See, e.g.*, Matthew Purdy, *Workplace Murders Provoke Lawsuits and Better Security*, N.Y. TIMES, Feb. 14, 1994, at A1, col. 4 (nat. ed.).

188. Harry Philo, *Revoke the Legal License to Kill Construction Workers*, 19 DE PAUL L. REV. 1 (1969); *To Promote Health and Safety* at 38–76 (testimony of Harry Philo).

189. H.R. REP. No. 1051, 100th Cong., 2d Sess. (1988).

190. *OSHA Penalties and Procedures: Hearing Before the Subcomm. on Labor of the Senate Labor & Human Resources Comm.*, 101st Cong., 2d Sess. 8 (S. Hrg. 101–390, 1990) (Rep. Lantos).

191. 29 U.S.C. § 666(e) (imprisonment of a 6 months and 1 year for repeat offenders).

192. Robert McFadden, *U.S. Won't Bring Criminal Charges in Building Collapse in Which 28 Died*, N.Y. TIMES, Nov. 20, 1988, § 1, at 38, col. 1 (Lexis). On the failure of the U.S. Dept. of Justice vigorously to prosecute employers under OSHA's criminal provision, see JOSEPH KINNEY & ROSALIE DAY, THE RISING WAVE: DEATH AND INJURY AMONG HIGH RISK WORKERS IN THE 1980s, at 13–15 (1987); William Glaberson, *States Are Toppling Workplace-Injury Convictions*, N.Y. TIMES, Sept. 19, 1988, at 1, col. 4 (nat. ed.).

193. *The OSHA Criminal Penalty Reform Act: Hearing Before the Subcomm. on Labor fo the Senate Comm. on Labor & Human Resources*, 102d Cong., 1st Sess. 7 (1991).

194. *See, e.g.*, SUBCOMMITTEE ON LABOR OF THE SENATE COMMITTEE ON LABOR AND PUBLIC WELFARE, 92D CONG., 1ST SESS., LEGISLATIVE HISTORY OF THE OCCUPATIONAL SAFETY AND HEALTH ACT OF 1970 (S. 2193, P.L. 91–596) iii (Comm. Print 1971) (foreword by Senator Harrison Williams, one of the eponymous sponsors of OSHA). *But see* NIOSH, FATAL INJURIES TO WORKERS at iii (foreword by J. Donald Millar, director of NIOSH).

195. U.S. BLS, Census of Fatal Occupational Injuries (unpublished data made available to author, Mar. 23, 1994). On the international trend toward lower fatality levels in the wake of the tertiarization of advanced economies, see OECD EMPLOYMENT OUTLOOK, July 1989, at 139, 142.

196. *Construction Safety, Health and Education Improvement Act of 1989* at 2 (Sen. Dodd). *See also* John Rekus, *Safety in the Trenches*, OCCUPATIONAL HEALTH AND SAFETY, Feb. 1992, at 26; William Schriver, *Study of Fatalities in the Construction Industry*, SURV. BUS., Summer/ Fall 1993, at 45.

197. *Legislative Hearings on H.R. 1063* at 243 (testimony of Dr. Knut Ringen on Laborers' Union membership in Indiana).

198. NIOSH, ALERT: REQUEST FOR ASSISTANCE IN PREVENTING HOMICIDE IN THE WORK-PLACE 4 (Pub. No. 93–109, 1993).

199. Cost-conscious firms appear much more enthusiastic about such costless "psychological techniques as hoisting the American flag . . . [which] inspires tidier premises, contributing to fewer accidents." Robert Hershey, Jr., *In Mississippi, a Clue to Low-Inflation Economics*, N.Y. TIMES, May 31, 1994, at A1, col. 2, at C2, col. 4 (nat. ed.).

200. 1 CARROLL DAUGHERTY, LABOR PROBLEMS IN AMERICAN INDUSTRY 117–19 (1944 [1931]); Robert Smith, *An Analysis of Work Injuries in Manufacturing Industry*, in 3 SUPPLE-MENTAL STUDIES FOR THE NATIONAL COMMISSION ON STATE WORKMEN'S COMPENSATION LAWS 9, 20, 23 (1973).

201. Nordheimer, *Pressure of Costs Drives Some Contractors to Stress Worker Safety* (quoting risk management consultant).

202. J.-M. CLERC, INTRODUCTION TO WORKING CONDITIONS AND ENVIRONMENT 29 (1985).

203. U.S. OCCUPATIONAL SAFETY & HEALTH ADMIN., CONSTRUCTION ACCIDENTS: THE WORKERS' COMPENSATION DATA BASE 1985–1988, at 15, 34 (1992).

204. U.S. BLS, Bull. 2252: INJURIES TO CONSTRUCTION LABORERS 4–5, tab. 11 at 16 (1986).

205. U.S. OCCUPATIONAL SAFETY & HEALTH ADMIN., CONSTRUCTION LOST-TIME INJURIES: THE U.S. ARMY CORPS OF ENGINEERS DATA BASE 1984–1988, at x, xi, 2, 8, 21, 41–42 (1992). The Army Corps of Engineers' safety program, which is imposed on the private contractors working for it and reportedly results in the lower accident rate, casts doubt on the claim that "no bosses' government body is going to interfere with the speed with which any boss decides it must make profit." *Capitalism Kills 51 Workers*, CHALLENGE, May 10, 1978, at 5.

206. Swen Kjaer & Max Kossoris, *Causes and Prevention of Accidents in the Construction Industry, 1939*, 51 MONTHLY LAB. REV. 935, 936 (1940).

207. 1 DAUGHERTY, LABOR PROBLEMS IN AMERICAN INDUSTRY at 105.

208. BUNDESMINISTERIUM FÜR INNERDEUTSCHE BEZIEHUNGEN, DEUTSCHLAND 1971, at 169 (n.d. [1971]).

209. John Conti, *Coal-Mine Study Shows Record Can Be Improved When Firms Really Try*, WALL ST. J., Jan. 18, 1973, at 1, col. 6, at 20, col. 3.

210. G. Collins, *Construction Safety*, in U.S. BUREAU OF LABOR STANDARDS, Bull. 243: PROCEEDINGS OF THE PRESIDENT'S CONFERENCE ON OCCUPATIONAL SAFETY 197, 199 (1962).

211. U.S. BLS, Bulletin No. 700: INDUSTRIAL-INJURY STATISTICS (1942); MAX KOSSORIS & FRANK McELROY, *Industrial Injuries in the United States During World War II*, 57 MONTHLY LAB. REV. 865 (1943).

212. *See* James Robinson, *The Rising Long-Term Trend in Occupational Injury Rates*, 78 AM. J. PUB. HEALTH 276 (1988).

213. INTERNATIONAL LABOUR OFFICE, INTERNATIONAL LABOUR CONFERENCE, 73RD SESSION, 1987: REPORT V (1): SAFETY AND HEALTH IN CONSTRUCTION 6 (1986).

214. Nordheimer, *Pressure of Costs Drives Some Contractors to Stress Worker Safety.*

215. Max Kossoris, *Industrial Injuries and the Business Cycle*, 46 MONTHLY LAB. REV. 579, 593–94 (1938).

216. *Work Injuries in 1948: Preliminary Estimates*, 68 MONTHLY LAB. REV. 289 (1949); James Robinson & Glenn Shor, *Business-Cycle Influences on Work-Related Disability in Construction and Manufacturing,*" 67 MILLBANK Q. 92 (Supp. 2, Pt. 1, 1989).

217. *See* U.S. DEPT. OF COMMERCE, SEASONAL OPERATION IN THE CONSTRUCTION INDUSTRIES: SUMMARY OF REPORT AND RECOMMENDATIONS OF A COMMITTEE OF THE PRESIDENT'S CONFERENCE ON UNEMPLOYMENT vi (1924) (customs fixed in preindustrial period rather than bad weather is the principal cause of seasonality).

218. U.S. BLS, INJURIES TO CONSTRUCTION LABORERS at 1; Norman Root & Michael Hoefer, *The First Work-Injury Data Available from New BLS Study*, MONTHLY LAB. REV., Jan. 1979, at 76, tab. 3 at 79 (1976 data from maryland).

219. *To Promote Health and Safety in the Building Trades and Construction Industry: Hearings Before the Select Comm. on Labor of the House Comm. on Education and Labor*, 91st Cong., 1st Sess. 35 (1969) (statement of John Lyons, general president, Int'l Ass'n of Bridge, Structural and Ornamental Ironworkers).

220. ASHFORD, CRISIS IN THE WORKPLACE at 46. *See also* Robert Smith, *The Feasibility of an "Injury Tax" Approach to Occupational Safety*, 38 LAW & CONTEMP. PROBS. 730 (1974).

221. Walter Oi, *On the Economics of Industrial Safety*, 38 LAW & CONTEMP. PROBS. 669, 680 (1974).

222. Pub. L. No. 91–173, 83 Stat. 742 (1969); Ben Franklin, *Safety Comes to the Mines a Century Late*, N.Y. TIMES, Jan. 4, 1970, § 4, at 3, col. 1.

223. Federal Mine Safety and Health Act of 1977, Pub. L. 95–164, 91 Stat. 1290 (1977) (codified at 30 U.S.C. §§ 801–962 (1988); Barry Newman, *Silver-Mine Disaster Prompts Fight on Laws Tightening Safety Rules*, WALL ST. J., Oct. 26, 1972, at 1, col. 6; S. REP. No. 181, 95th Cong., 1st Sess. 3–4, *reprinted in* 1977 U.S. CODE CONG. & ADMIN. NEWS 3401, 3403–3404.

224. On the continuity of such weak enforcement under the Mine Safety Act, see Burt Schorr, *Coal-Safety Violators Get Bargain-Rate Fines from Bureau of Mines*, WALL ST. J., July 28, 1971, at 1, col. 6; Rand Guffey, *Enforcing of New Law Bogs Down, Stirring Uproar in Coalfields*, WALL ST. J., June 25, 1970, at 1, col. 6.

225. *See, e.g.*, Walsh-Healey Government Contracts Act, ch. 881, § 1(e), 49 Stat. 2036, 2037 (1936) (codified at 41 U.S.C. § 35(e) (1988)); Service Contract Labor Standards Act, Pub. L. No. 89–286, § 2(a)(3) (1965) (codified at 41 U.S.C. § 351(a)(3) (1988)); Longshore and Harbor Workers' Compensation Act, Pub. L. No. 85–742, 72 Stat. 835 (1958) (codified at 33 U.S.C. § 941 (1988)) (enjoining employers to maintain "reasonably safe employment" for employees on the navigable waters of the United States and authorizing Secretary of Labor to issue regulations to protect such employees).

226. Walter Rugaber, *Records Show That Lax Government Regulations Allow Occupational Hazards to Grow*, N.Y. TIMES, Jan. 2, 1970, at 17, col. 1

227. U.S. BLS, Bull. 1656: COMPENSATION IN THE CONSTRUCTION INDUSTRY: EMPLOYMENT PATTERNS, UNION SCALES, AND EARNINGS 23 (1970).

228. *Federal Construction Safety: Hearings Before the Subcomm. on Labor of the Senate Comm. on Labor and Public Welfare*, 91st Cong., 1st Sess. 8 (1969).

229. *Construction Safety: Hearings Before the Select Subcomm. on Labor of the House Comm. on Education and Labor*, 90th Cong., 1st & 2d Sess. 6 (1968) (C.J. Haggerty).

230. BERMAN, DEATH ON THE JOB at 76.

231. *Construction Safety* at 44.

232. Byron Calame, *Job-Hazard Law Spurs Complaints from Firms on Cost of Safeguards*, WALL ST. J., Dec. 1, 1971, at 1, col. 1, at 19, col. 3. Engels had noticed 125 years earlier

that the necessity of working fast caused accidents. FRIEDRICH ENGELS, DIE LAGE DER ARBEITENDEN KLASSE IN ENGLAND, in 2 KARL MARX [&] FRIEDRICH ENGELS, WERKE 225, 388 (1957 [1844]).

233. *See* STUDENTERFRONTENS ARBEJDSMEDICINGRUPPE, MALER RAPPORTEN: EN FORELBIG RAPPORT OM SUNDHEDSFARERNE I MALERFAGET 24 (Aarhus: Studenrrådet, n.d. [ca. 1971]) (discussing masks for painters); OECD EMPLOYMENT OUTLOOK, July 1989, at 137; TOM DWYER, LIFE AND DEATH AT WORK: INDUSTRIAL ACCIDENTS AS A CASE OF SOCIALLY PRODUCED ERROR 104–105 (1991).

234. *Legislative Hearings on H.R. 1063* at 28 (testimony of Greg Denton, director of safety, Fluor-Daniel and chair, Associated Builders & Contractors, Safety Comm.).

235. *Legislative Hearings on H.R. 1063* at 218 (statement of Sigurd Lucassen)

236. H.R. 1063, § 4(a), H.R. Rep. No. 662, 102d Cong., 2d Sess. 4 (1991).

237. *Legislative Hearings on H.R. 1063* at 36 (testimony of Ira Norris).

238. *Legislative Hearings on the Construction Safety, Health, and Education Improvement Act of 1990* at 62–63 (statement of Neil Norman, president elect, National Society of Professional Engineers). *See also id.* at 353 (testimony of J. Donald Millar, director, NIOSH); LaBar, *Breaking New Ground in Construction Safety* at 63.

239. The desolate state of industrial injury statistics in the United States corresponded, at least until the advent of OSHA and NIOSH, to the lack of a national occupational injury and disease prevention policy or an appropriate research program. For examples of the much more advanced European research in construction safety and health, see JAN WAHLBERG, YRKESHUDSJUKDOMAR HOS BYGGNADSARBETARE (Byggnadsindustrins Forskningsrapporter och Uppsatser No. 11; n.d. [1968]); SEVED LINDQUIST, HÖRSELSKADOR HOS BYGGNADSARBETARE (Byggnadsindustrins Forskningsrapporter och Uppsatser No. 15; n.p., n.d. [1969]); JAN KRONLUND, P BYGGET: ARBETSPSYKOLOGISKA STUDIER I BYGGNADSINDUSTRIN (1969); III. INTERNATIONALES SYMPOSIUM ARBEITSHYGIENE UND ARBEITSSCHUTZ IM BAUWESEN (1972]).

240. 29 U.S.C. § 654 (a)(1) (1988).

241. 29 C.F.R. § 1910.151 (1992). The term "in near proximity" survived a joint challenge as to vagueness by the OSHA Review Commission and an employer; Brennan v. Occupational Safety and Health Review Commission and Santa Fe Trail Transport Co., 505 F.2d 869 (10th Cir. 1974).

242. 40 U.S.C. § 333 (1988).

243. 29 C.F.R. § 1926.50(b) & (c) (1988).

244. David Graulich, *Company or Patient? Corporate Physicians Torn by Dual Loyalty,* WALL ST. J., Oct. 3, 1975, at 1, col. 1.

245. U.S. BLS, Bull. 1830: OCCUPATIONAL INJURIES AND ILLNESSES BY INDUSTRY, 1972, at 6–9, 98 (1974).

246. Hugh Conway, Jennifer Simmons, & Terry Talbert, *The Occupational Safety and Health Administration's 1990–1991 Survey of Occupational Medical Surveillance Prevalence and Type of Current Practices,* 35 J. OCCUPATIONAL MED. 659, tab. 2 at 662 (1993).

247. U.S. BLS, Bull. 1830: OCCUPATIONAL INJURIES AND ILLNESSES BY INDUSTRY, 1972 at 6.

248. *See* SABINE KAISER, GEWERKSCHAFTEN UND MEDIZIN 2: BETRIEBSÄRTZLICHE VERSORGUNG IN DER BRD UND IN ANDEREN EG-STAATEN 72–84 (1973).

249. See OECD, EMPLOYMENT OUTLOOK, July 1989, at 139.

250. *See* HANS-ULRICH DEPPE, INDUSTRIEARBEIT UND MEDIZIN: EIN BEITRAG ZUR SOZIOLOGIE MEDIZINISCHER INSTITUTIONEN AM BEISPIEL DES WERKSÄRTZLICHEN DIENSTES IN DER BRD 113–14, 151 (1973).

251. DOROTHY NELKIN & MICHAEL BROWN, WORKERS AT RISK: VOICES FROM THE WORKPLACE 91 (1984) (interview with chemical operator in food processing plant).

252. James Chelius, *The Control of Industrial Accidents: Economic Theory and Empirical Evidence,* 38 LAW & CONTEMP. PROBS. 700, 702 (1974).

253. *See, e.g.,* Robert McLean, Wayne Wending, & Paul Neergard, *Compensating Wage*

Differentials for Hazardous Work: An Empirical Analysis, Q. REV. ECON. & BUS., Autumn 1978, at 97.

254. ADAM SMITH, AN INQUIRY INTO THE NATURE AND CAUSES OF THE WEALTH OF NATIONS 100, 99 (1937 [1776]). "In trades which are known to be very unwholesome, the wages of labour are always remarkably high." *Id.* at 110.

255. *See, e.g.*, W. RORABAUGH, THE CRAFT APPRENTICE: FROM FRANKLIN TO THE MACHINE AGE IN AMERICA 131 (1986) (quoting a mid-nineteenth-century journeyman). Why under these circumstances the non-Smithian outcome is "unfortunate[] for all concerned" including the employer is unclear. LAWRENCE BACOW, BARGAINING FOR JOB SAFETY AND HEALTH 52 (1981 [1980]).

256. K. WEDDERBURN, THE WORKER AND THE LAW 419 (3d ed. 1986 [1965]).

257. For speculation as to why such reported cases appeared so late, see BARTRIP & BURMAN, THE WOUNDED SOLDIERS OF INDUSTRY at 24–25, 103–105.

258. Murray v. South Carolina R.R., 26 S.C.L. (1 McMul.) 385, 402 (1841).

259. Farwell v. Boston & Worcester R.R., 45 Mass. (4 Metc.) 49, 57 (1842).

260. JOHN STUART MILL, THE PRINCIPLES OF POLITICAL ECONOMY 388 (W. Ashley ed. 1926 [1852]).

261. Thrussell v. Handyside, 20 Q.B.D. 359, 364 (1888).

262. For a similar approach, see SIDNEY WEBB & BEATRICE WEBB, INDUSTRIAL DEMOCRACY 356–57 (1920 [1897]).

263. ALFRED MARSHALL, PRINCIPLES OF ECONOMICS 464 (8th ed. 1969 [1890]).

264. 42 CONG. REC. 1347 (1908).

265. [NEW YORK STATE COMMISSION ON EMPLOYERS LIABILITY], MINUTES OF EVIDENCE 17 (1910).

266. [NEW YORK STATE COMM'N ON EMPLOYERS LIABILITY], REPORT at 7.

267. "[T]he human being as the bearer of labor performance is not only a factor of production, but, with his wishes and purposes, the starting point and goal of all economic activity in general." ERICH SCHNEIDER, EINFÜHRUNG IN DIE WIRTSCHAFTSTHEORIE, II. TEIL 374 (1967).

268. *See e.g.*, PAUL SAMUELSON, ECONOMICS 579 (9th ed. 1973).

269. W. VISCUSI, EMPLOYMENT HAZARDS: AN INVESTIGATION OF MARKET PERFORMANCE 271 (1979).

270. *See* Oi, *On the Economics of Industrial Safety* at 695 n.70 ("A worker could, conceivably, go from plant to plant and examine the posted annual summaries [of injuries required by OSHA] to see which plant had the best industrial safety record last year").

271. WILLIAM PROSSER, HANDBOOK OF THE LAW OF TORTS 506 (1941).

272. VISCUSI, RISK BY CHOICE at 45–46.

273. JAMES ROBINSON, TOIL AND TOXICS: WORKPLACE STRUGGLES AND POLITICAL STRATEGIES FOR OCCUPATIONAL HEALTH 75–94 (1991).

274. Adna Weber, *Employers' Liability and Accident Insurance*, 18 POL. SCI. Q. 256, 258–59 (1902). *See also* [NEW YORK STATE COMM'N], REPORT at 7.

275. FRANK LEWIS, STATE INSURANCE: A SOCIAL AND INDUSTRIAL NEED 81 (1909).

276. J. Leigh, *No Evidence of Compensating Wages for Occupational Fatalities*, 30 INDUS. REL. 382 (1991).

277. VISCUSI, EMPLOYMENT HAZARDS at 250.

278. Robert Smith, *Compensating Wage Differentials and Public Policy: A Review*, 32 INDUS. & LAB. REL. REV. 339, 344–46 (1979).

279. Ronald Ehrenberg, *Workers' Compensation, Wages, and the Risk of Injury*, in NEW PERSPECTIVES IN WORKERS' COMPENSATION 71, 79–81 (John Burton, Jr. ed., 1988).

280. *See, e.g.*, REPORT OF THE NATIONAL COMMISSION ON STATE WORKMEN'S COMPENSATION LAWS 18 (1972); Monroe Berkowitz, *Workmen's Compensation Income Benefits: Their Adequacy*

and Equity, in 1 SUPPLEMENTAL STUDIES FOR THE NATIONAL COMMISSION ON STATE WORK-MEN'S COMPENSATION LAWS 189, 200–204 (1973); EDWARD BERKOWITZ, DISABLED POLICY: AMERICA'S PROGRAMS FOR THE HANDICAPPED 33–40 (1989 [1987]). Farming occupations accounted for less than 3 percent of employment but 11 percent of fatalities. Toscano & Windau, *Fatal Work Injuries,* tab. 5 at 44.

281. Richard Frenkel, W. Priest, & Nicholas Ashford, *Occupational Safety and Health: A Report on Worker Perceptions,* MONTHLY LAB. REV., Sept. 1980, at 11.

282. NELKIN & BROWN, WORKERS AT RISK at 92.

283. *Brutal, Mindless Labor Remains a Daily Reality for Millions in the U.S.,* WALL ST. J., July 16, 1971, at 1, col. 6.

284. ROBINSON, TOIL AND TOXICS at 96–105.

285. Craig Olson, *An Analysis of Wage Differentials Received by Workers on Dangerous Jobs,* 16 J. HUMAN RESOURCES 167, 185 (1981). ·

286. James Robinson, *Hazard Pay in Unsafe Jobs: Theory, Evidence, and Policy Implications,* 64 MILBANK Q. 650, 663 (1986). *See also* Jeff Biddle & Gary Zarkin, *Worker Preferences and Market Compensation for Job Risk,* 70 REV. ECON. & STATISTICS 660, tab. 5 at 666 (1988) (compensation required to make union workers indifferent to a 1/100 increase in probability of injury almost six times greater than for nonunion worker). Significantly, the two relatively highly paid unskilled jobs that *Wall Street Journal* reporters found to be dangerous to safety (token seller in New York City subway system) and health (tunnel patrolman in New York City) were in the public sector and unionized. *Monotonous Labor Is Torturous for Some, 'My Thing' for Others,* WALL ST. J., July 22, 1971, at 1, col. 6.

287. William Dickens, *Differences Between Risk Premiums in Union and Nonunion Wages and the Case for Occupational Safety Regulation,* 74 AM. ECON. REV. 320 (1984).

288. GUIDO CALABRESI, THE COSTS OF ACCIDENTS: A LEGAL AND ECONOMIC ANALYSIS 207 n.7 (1971 [1970]). For a description of the implementation of unusually strong union safety and health programs at several large employers, see BACOW, BARGAINING FOR JOB SAFETY AND HEALTH at 60–87.

289. Kisner & Fosbroke, *Injury Hazards in the Construction Industry* at 140–41. The figure for non-construction laborers is estimated because it had to be read off a graph.

290. Toscano & Windau, *Fatal Work Injuries,* tab. 5 at 44.

291. The union premium for wage rates among construction laborers ranged between 40 and 70 percent in the early 1970s. U.S. BLS, Bull. 1853: INDUSTRY WAGE SURVEY: CONTRACT CONSTRUCTION, SEPTEMBER 1972, at 6 (1975); U.S. BLS, Bull. 1911: INDUSTRY WAGE SURVEY: CONTRACT CONSTRUCTION, SEPTEMBER 1973, at 5 (1976).

292. Among all full-time laborers (that is, handlers, equipment cleaners, helpers, and laborers), the union premium on median weekly earnings ranged between 58 percent and 76 percent between 1983 and 1992. U.S. BLS, Bull. 2340: HANDBOOK OF LABOR STATISTICS, tab. 42 at 163–68 (1989); EMPLOYMENT & EARNINGS, Jan. 1992, at 231; EMPLOYMENT & EARNINGS, Jan. 1993, at 241.

293. Calculated according to U.S. BLS, Rep. 417: SELECTED EARNINGS AND DEMOGRAPHIC CHARACTERISTICS OF UNION MEMBERS, 1970, tab. 6 at 13 (1972).

294. U.S. BLS, Rep. 556: EARNINGS AND OTHER CHARACTERISTICS OF ORGANIZED WORK-ERS, MAY 1977, tab. 10 at 28 (1979); U.S. BLS, Bull. 2105: EARNINGS AND OTHER CHARAC-TERISTICS OF ORGANIZED WORKERS, MAY 1980, tab. 10 at 30 (1981). The 1977 and 1980 results are not comparable with those for 1970.

295. For early welfare economics recognition of the phenomenon in a different context, see A. Henderson, *Consumer's Surplus and the Compensating Variation,* 8 REV. ECON. STUD. 117 (1941).

296. Mark Kelman, *Consumption Theory, Production Theory, and Ideology in the Coase Theorem,"* 52 S. CAL. L. REV. 669, 682 (1979); Jack Knetsch & J. Sinden, *Willingness to Pay and Compensation Demanded as Experimental Evidence of an Unexpected Disparity in Measures of Value,* 99 Q.J. ECON. 507 (1984); Jack Knetsch, *The Endowment Effect and Evidence of*

Nonreversible Indifference Curves, 79 AM. ECON. REV. 1277 (1989); Herbert Hovenkamp, *Legal Policy and the Endowment Effect*, 20 J. LEG. STUD. 225 (1991).

297. Shelby Gerking, Menno de Haan, & William Schulze, *The Marginal Value of Job Safety: A Contingent Valuation Study*, 1 J. RISK & UNCERTAINTY 188, 192 (1988). Those who chose to respond to this lengthy and complex mail questionnaire were probably disproportionately high-income persons in low-risk jobs. The fact that almost one-quarter of respondents were willing to assume a riskier job without any monetary inducement suggests that they may have failed to understand the questionnaire. Finally, the questions themselves, which referred to a hypothetical and vague external comparison with the risks attaching to other jobs, lacked the concreteness of an internal comparison with the respondent's own current work.

298. MCGARITY & SHAPIRO, WORKERS AT RISK at 273.

299. *See* Herbert Hovenkamp, *Marginal Utility and the Coase Theorem*, 75 CORNELL L. REV. 783, 798–804 (1990).

300. *See, e.g.*, Alan Marin & George Psacharopolous, *The Reward for Risk in the Labor Market: Evidence for the United Kingdom and a Reconciliation with Other Studies*, 90 J. POL. ECON. 827, 834–36 (1982).

301. Hovenkamp, *Marginal Utility and the Coase Theorem* at 804.

302. *See* MAURICE DOBB, WAGES 140–41 (1966 [1928]); MARTIN WEITZMAN, THE SHARE ECONOMY: CONQUERING STAGFLATION 121 (1984).

303. ECONOMIC REPORT OF THE PRESIDENT 179, 195–201 (1987).

304. *Legislative Hearings on the Construction Safety, Health, and Education Improvement Act of 1990* at 490.

305. 29 C.F.R. § 1977.12 (1993); Whirlpool Corp. v. Marshall, 445 U.S. 1 (1980). *See generally*, James Atleson, *Threats to Safety and Health: Employee Self-Help Under the NLRA*, 59 MINN. L. REV. 647 (1975). On the somewhat less risky choices facing workers under a strong union contract, see BACOW, BARGAINING FOR JOB SAFETY AND HEALTH at 74, 141 n.19.

306. STANLEY LEBERGOTT, MANPOWER IN ECONOMIC GROWTH: THE AMERICAN RECORD SINCE 1860, at 250–51 (1964).

307. For experiments showing that some workers will decline certain kinds of work (such as handling TNT) regardless of the wage premium, see W. Viscusi & Charles O'Connor, *Adaptive Responses to Chemical Labeling: Are Workers Bayesian Decision Makers?* 74 AM. ECON. REV. 943, 949, 953 (1984).

308. Friedman & Ladinsky, *Social Change and the Law of Industrial Accidents* at 71.

309. WILLIAM HARD ET AL., INJURED IN THE COURSE OF DUTY 37, 38 (1910 [1908]).

310. Franklin, *Safety Comes to the Mines a Century Late*.

311. Anthony Bale, Compensation Crisis at 54.

312. *See* William Dickens, *Occupational Safety and Health Regulation and Economic Theory*, in LABOR ECONOMICS: MODERN VIEWS 133, 135 (William Darity, Jr. ed. 1984).

313. 1 DAUGHERTY, LABOR PROBLEMS IN AMERICAN INDUSTRY at 117–19.

314. K. WILLIAM KAPP, THE SOCIAL COSTS OF PRIVATE ENTERPRISE 48–49 (1971 [1950]).

315. U.S. BLS, Bull. No. 304: PROCEEDINGS OF THE EIGHTH ANNUAL MEETING OF THE INTERNATIONAL ASSOCIATION OF INDUSTRIAL ACCIDENT BOARDS AND COMMISSIONS at 62 (A. Pillsbury).

316. KAPP, SOCIAL COSTS at 65.

317. [NEW YORK STATE COMM'N], REPORT at 133.

318. LEBERGOTT, MANPOWER IN ECONOMIC GROWTH at 250–51. Such entrepreneurial calculations appear to be anticipatory corroboration of a much later claim that: "Under capitalism there are no accidents—there is only murder of one class by another." "Capitalism Kills 51 Workers.'

319. A recent revision of the Internal Revenue Code takes the distinction between capital and human capital to its illogical conclusion. Congress included among the intangibles with

respect to which firms are entitled to take amortization deductions a "workforce in place." Omnibus Budget Reconciliation Act of 1993, Pub. L. No. 103–66, § 13261, 1993 U.S. CODE CONG. & ADMIN. NEWS (107 Stat.) 312, 533 (to be codified at 26 U.S.C. § 197). Thus a firm may amortize over a 15-year period the portion of the purchase price of a business attributable to the "experience, education, or training . . . of a highly skilled workforce," although neither the individual members of that purchased workforce nor any other workers are entitled to take amortization deductions for the value of their cash outlays for that human capital, which they embody. H.R. CONF. REP. NO. 213, 103d Cong., 1st Sess. 675, reprinted in 1993 U.S. CODE CONG. & ADMIN. NEWS 1088, 1364.

320. KAPP, SOCIAL COSTS at 49–5.

321. 3 MARX, DAS KAPITAL at 87–107. Not among the incentives that capital has in disregarding its workers' welfare is the "expropriation" of their health. Vicente Navarro, *The Labor Process and Health: A Historical Materialist Approach*, 12 INT'L J. HEALTH SERVICES 5, 13 (1982). Since the workers' loss of their health is not accompanied by its centralization on capital's side because it has been destroyed rather than transferred, such rhetorical flourishes in fact invert Marx's use of *expropriation*. 1 KARL MARX, DAS KAPITAL: KRITIK DER POLITISCHEN ÖKONOMIE, in 23 MARX & ENGELS, WERKE 789–91 (1962 [3d ed. 1883]).

322. *See, e.g.*, W. CARSON, THE OTHER PRICE OF BRITAIN'S OIL: SAFETY AND CONTROL IN THE NORTH SEA 42–79 (1982); William Graebner, *Doing the World's Unhealthy Work: The Fiction of Free Choice*, HASTINGS CENTER REPORT, Aug. 1984, at 28.